MAI
IN SUSSEX

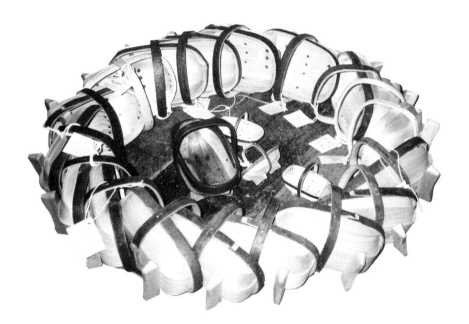

Sussex Crafts and Industries Past and Present

Elizabeth Wright

S.B. Publications

**Dedicated to my beloved daughter
Jacqueline Dendy-Sadler**

First published in 2000 by S B Publications
19 Grove Road, Seaford, Sussex BN25 1TP
01323 893498
fax 01323 893860
sales@sbpublications.swinternet.co.uk

ISBN 1 85770 195

Typeset by JEM Editorial, Lewes
JEMedit@AOL.com

Printed by Tansleys the Printers
19 Broad Street
Seaford
Sussex BN25 1LS
01323 891019

CONTENTS

FOREWORD

I have lived in Sussex for most of my life. It is a county I love and the very name Sussex conjures up images of pastoral scenes, picturesque lanes and enchanting villages. Kipling was inspired to write about its 'blunt, bow-headed, whale-backed downs', the green undulations that hug the coastline and drop dramatically into the sea at Beachy Head. For most people, this corner of England is best known today for its tourism and agriculture. But Sussex has had its great moments as an industrialised county when the manufacture of iron, glass and guns brought immense prosperity to the area. Small, quaint businesses flourished too. Pullinger's Selsey Mouse Traps, Burstow's Penny Four-Farthing cycles, Harmer's unique terracotta plaques, Herstmonceux's trug baskets and Bexhill's coal mines.

When I started researching for this book, gathering information on past and present industries that were uniquely Sussex, I found many interesting and fascinating businesses. The more I delved, the more I found. In the end I had to make a hard decision what to put in and, reluctantly, what to leave out. Those contained in these pages are a distilled essence of twenty-three varied Sussex industries and the people involved with them.

Elizabeth Wright
2000

ACKNOWLEDGMENTS

Colin Davies, formerly of Sussex Hand Made Brick Ltd; Hugh Parker of Caffyns plc; Simon Tilbury; Gray-Nicolls; Harold Beeney; Jonathan Chiswell Jones of JCJ Pottery; Fiona Richardson of Brickhurst Pottery; Richard and Margaret Buss; John Andree of Solaglass (Eastbourne); Sheila Stamford of Pilkington Glass Museum; Sarah Page of The Truggery, Herstmonceux; Mollie Reed; Robin M Tuppen of Thomas Smith's Trug Shop, Herstmonceux; the staff of Anne of Cleves House, Lewes, and Lewes Castle; Dave Watson of Isetta Owners Club of Great Britain.

1

PENNY FOUR-FARTHINGS CYCLES

Architect Henry Burstow of Horsham was a talented inventor, and in the 1880s he took the idea of the penny farthing, the velocipede, a stage further. He designed a carrier cycle, which he called the Centre Cycle, with five wheels, two small wheels in the front and two behind with the driving wheel in the centre. By lifting handles the two front or two back wheels could be raised, or all four at one time, leaving only the driving wheel on the ground.

This unusual machine, nicknamed 'hen and chickens', attracted a great deal of media attention. The *Sussex Evening Times* of September 29, 1881, reported: 'At the King's Road Skating Rink, yesterday, this newly invented machine was exhibited in the presence of several well known local gentleman. This velocipede will occupy a place in the cycling world quite independently of the present make of bi- and tri-cycles. It fulfils a want long-felt of a medium class machine, many of the younger generation preferring something risky and the elderly ones all the safety they can possibly get.

'The safety is such that even the novice can ride and maintain his equilibrium. It will also go over any obstacles to be met in the roadway, as each wheel in turn rises as occasion desires. By pressure on the handles, which resemble the 'governor' of the bicycle, the centre, or driving wheel can be raised, the machine thus having independent action on the four wheels. By this means the machine can be started in any position, as the dead centres are overcome.

'The rider sits entirely over his work, and is thus enabled to use his whole weight for driving. All five wheels assist in steering, the driving wheel lying over towards the centre of the circle described. We believe smaller curves can be made on this than on any other machine previously seen.

'The extreme width is a trifle over two feet, therefore allowing it to enter any ordinary doorway. One of the advantages to be derived is the elevated position gained, as it enables one to have a good view of the surrounding country as he journeys along the road.

'The inventor of this unique and ingenious specimen of velocipede – Mr. Edward Burstow, of Horsham, a gentleman whose inventive powers have been in many other instances most successfully employed – deserves great credit for producing such a perfectly novel and carefully thought out machine, which entirely differs from anything previously introduced. The Centre Cycle was decidedly appreciated by those gentlemen who received an invitation to be

Burstow's Centre Cycle also known as the "Hen and Chickens" cycle, in use by the General Post Office in 1882

present at the Rink yesterday, and frequent were the expressions of admiration of the machine's simplicity of construction.

'Many who had never ridden a bicycle were riding about the Rink with apparent ease and enjoyment. These machines, will, we believe, remain on view here for some days longer, and anyone interested in cycling would do well to view them. No arrangements have yet been made for sale, but as soon as they are put on the market, no doubt every information will be given to the public.'

It would appear that the invitation to 'the well known local gentlemen' was for Edward Burstow to obtain financial support to improve and exploit his invention. Indeed, he must have been successful because soon afterwards the Centre Cycle Company was formed.

On November 21, 1882, the *Sussex Express* reported: 'Mr. Burstow of Horsham, appears to have supplied a great want by the invention of his patent Centre-cycle, which bids fair to be of a great utility in the carrying out of the new parcels post system. On Friday, by permission of the park directorate, the National Postal Congress, now sitting at Eastbourne, made some experiments in locomotion, with machines etc. in Devonshire Park.

'In addition to many of the chief officials of the Transit Department of the General Post Office, London, the attendance included Mr. Perry, postal surveyor of the South-Eastern District, and also the numerous postal delegates now in Eastbourne, from all the chief cities in England, Ireland, Scotland and Wales. These representatives were met at the park by Mr. R. Insoil (Chairman of the park directorate), Captain Holman (manager), Mr. G.A.Wallis, C.E. (engineer to the Duke of Devonshire), and other gentlemen. The meeting was held to make tests of the means of the parcel post delivery, and Mr. Burrows attended by special request.

'A number of lads in the postal service in Mid-Sussex also attended to give practical illustration of the machines, already in some cases adopted for the benefit of postmen and telegraph boys in the rural districts. During the afternoon almost every evolution of which the Centre-cycle are capable was exhibited to the members of the Postal Congress by practised and unpractised riders. Many of the leading postal officials expressed themselves pleased with the machines.

'Capacious side and end baskets were attached to some of the machines, and it was explained that such receptacles might be heavily freighted with postal bags of parcels without interfering with the speed or endangering the safety of the riders. At the close of the somewhat lengthy experiments, Mr. Burstow was complimented by not a few of the postal officials upon his invention, and the question of its adoption as a means of rural conveyance was to be referred

Four postmen and a telegraph boy test-ride the 'hen and chickens'

to the Receptacle and Delivery Committee of the Congress at the Cavendish Hotel before the closing of the sitting.'

The GPO bought three machines on a trial basis but after intensive use they were rejected as not being durable enough and, said the service's surveyor, '. . . it is doubtful whether their use could be continued for any length of time without injury to the riders . . .' The postal service chose instead to use basket carrying tricycles.

A disappointed Edward Burstow appears to have ceased production of his special cycles after that decision.

2

ROPE-MAKING IN 'STRINGTOWN'

In Sussex, a county with a rich maritime heritage, there has always been a demand for ropes for its ships and boats. There is mention of ropemakers at Playden in 1572 and 1587, also in Rye in 1610, but Hailsham is well qualified to be called Stringtown, for although once a prosperous agricultural centre, much of the town's growth during the last two centuries can be credited to its rope- and string-making industry.

A journeyman saddler and collar maker, Thomas Burfield, moved to Hailsham in 1780 and set up business in the High Street. At first he bought in the cord for his business from dealers in London, but by 1807 he was making his own ropes, adapting a narrow passage behind his shop (where Woolworth now stands) for a rope walk.

As the business prospered, other walks, each about seventy-five yards long, were set up on land owned by the Burfield family. Originally, the ropes were make by hand in these walks. Spinners, usually outworkers, each carrying

The spinning walks in Mill Road in the late nineteenth century

9

The Burfield factory and rope walk in South Road a century ago

some thirty to forty pounds of hemp around their waists, would walk backwards, making and playing out the twine as they went, feeding it to a wheel turned by a 'spinning boy'. At intervals there were hooks on which to hang the completed yarn to prevent it becoming soiled.

Once a day or each week the spinners would take their completed ropes in wheelbarrows to the warehouse in the High Street, and collect their piece-work money along with a fresh supply of hemp.

George Green, a spinner from Staffordshire, was also as influential as Thomas Burfield in shaping the destiny of Hailsham. He worked as a spinner for Burfield until, in 1830, he set up his own rope-making business in the town. By 1846 both companies were turning out ropes, corn and twine as well as green hop sacks, flour bags, halters and harnesses for horses and oxen, webbing, clothes lines, mats and door mats.

'All the ropes for capital punishment used by the government at home and in the colonies are made in Hailsham,' said an article in *Cassells Magazine* in June 1898.

By 1871 more than 100 local people were employed in the rope industry, the majority being twine spinners, the rest hemp dressers and sack makers. Often whole families were earning a good living in the rope-making industry. Burfield, who died in 1874, was a respected businessman and a benevolent employer who made sure that children working in his factory attended school.

By the end of the century George Green's business was thriving more than Burfield's which, in 1903, became a limited company. Although there was a demand for Burfield products during the First World War, bringing about a small revival, the rope-making business of Burfield and Son declined and eventually was absorbed, with Green's, into the Hawkins and Tipson group.

Today, Marlow Ropes, in Diplocks Way, keeps up the tradition of rope-making in Hailsham.

The Burfield chimney remains, but today it serves as a symbol for the Burfield Park industrial estate

3

CAFFYNS' COACH BODIES

Caffyn is a name widely respected in Sussex, a name long associated with quality cars and quality service. It comes as no surprise, therefore, to discover that in 1927 the company received the Rolls Royce franchise to supply individually-made coach bodies for these prestigious cars.

There have been Caffyns living in Sussex since 1327. William Morris Caffyn was born in 1840 and joined his uncle Ebenezer Morris to learn the trade of 'Ironmonger, Tinman and Brazier', for which he was paid two shillings a week.

On May 19, 1865, William Morris opened his own shop in Meads Road, Eastbourne, offering his services as 'gas and hot water fitter, bell hanger, brass finisher and brazier,' and when he obtained a licence to store petroleum at the rear of the premises he added 'lamp and oil merchant' to his list.

His two sons, Harry Bruce and Percy Thomas, joined the firm in 1892 and a few years later opened an electrical domestic appliance business at 1 Church Street, Old Town, Eastbourne.

In the meantime, William Morris, besides carrying out the installation of

A Rolls Royce car body built by Caffyns in the 1920s

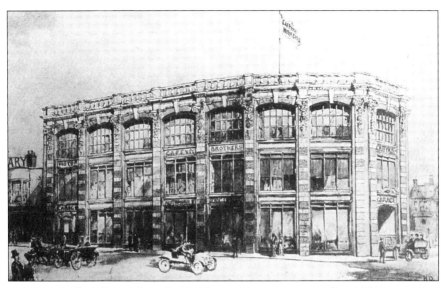

The Marine Parade, Eastbourne, garage, opened in 1906

electric lighting, was offering 'electric bells, telephones, gas fittings and repairs, tool dealers, cutlers and ironmongers'. Needing larger premises as the electrical side expanded, he took over an old shop at 12 The Colonnade, Eastbourne.

An event then occurred which had a significant effect on the future of the Caffyn family. As Harry said: 'One day a young fellow staying nearby came along with a four-cylinder Renault car (the first live axle car we had seen) and asked if he could stand it outside, or he would pay us for accommodation. The shop, having been a butchers, was fitted with wide sashes to draw up and when pushed up there was plenty of head room for a car to get under, but there was the bottom of the sill. This I cut away after dark without asking the landlord's permission, boarded over the gap, and in went the first car.'

There soon followed a request from the Queen's Hotel to store and polish some cars. Percy and Harry realised that the way forward was with the motor car and in 1903 they bought out their father for £1,800 and traded as Caffyn Brothers, converting the premises at 12 The Colonnade to hold four cars.

A year later it had been enlarged to hold sixteen cars and was called Caffyn's Garage.

From 1904 to 1905 the turnover from car sales was £300, and the Caffyn brothers were appointed agents for the General Accident Assurance Corporation. Initially they contracted out the work to local craftsmen.

13

COACHWORK
BY
CAFFYNS GARAGES
LTD

TRADESMAN'S
DELIVERY VAN

PIANOFORTE VAN

Special Low
Construction

A page from Caffyns' first coachwork catalogue in 1912. The top vehicle is on a Talbot car chassis, strengthened to take a commercial body. The lower van is on a Belsize commercial chassis with chain drive. Both vehicles had wooden wheels

QUOTATIONS & DESIGNS
FOR ANY TYPE OF BODY
ON APPLICATION

14

Caffyns' coachwork on display at the Olympia Motor Show in 1921

The brothers began to look around for larger premises capable of holding 100 cars and where sales, service and coachbuilding facilities could all be provided under one roof. They did not have far to look. A site nearby, on the corner of Marine Parade and Seaside Road, was turned into a fine garage.

The ironmongery shops were closed as all the firm's resources were pooled into the growing motor business. By 1906 there were forty-eight staff employed and in 1909 Caffyn Brothers became a public company and the name was changed to Caffyn's Garages Ltd.

The process of making the Rolls-Royce coachbodies began with the design being drawn to full scale, covering every detail right down to the last screw, on a large sheet of cartridge paper. The wood for the frame was ash, gathered from Sussex woodlands, stored until well seasoned and cut so that it tongued or dovetailed together with great accuracy. Caffyn's boasted that with such workmanship there was little chance of any body squeaks. Every stage of the bodywork was done at the Seaside Road garage by skilled carpenters, panel beaters and welders.

History came full circle when, in 1997, George Clark of Eastbourne, a skilled coachwork painter, who had worked for Caffyns (as the company is now known) for fifty-three years, was re-united with a 1933 Rolls Royce

George Clark and Tony Dannithorne with the 1933 Rolls Royce 20/25

20/25 which he had helped to make. The car had originally been bought by an Eastbourne resident and used regularly to commute to London. In the 1960s and 1970s it was to be found in Essex, then was it was auctioned and shipped out to the USA.

When the car was re-imported to Britain, Caffyns, knowing its history, bought it and, in 1994-95, under the guidance of Tony Donnithorne, Caffyns' Historic Vehicle Manager, it was restored to its original pristine condition.

George Clark was treated to a ride in the vehicle he had helped to create sixty-three years earlier. This Rolls is now the flagship of Caffyns' fleet of historic vehicles that are displayed at a number of events throughout the year.

4

BRICK MAKING

Had you lived in Sussex a century or two ago there would probably have been one near you – a brickyard that is. Nearly every parish had one. The subsoil in most of Sussex, apart from the chalky downland, is rich in the clays and sands that are ideal brickmaking materials.

In AD43 the conquering Romans brought with them a highly developed technique of brick and tile making. Over the next 300 years they built a number of army camps, fortifications and villas along the south coast and examples of their work can still be seen in the walls of Pevensey Castle. Here thin bricks have been used in bonding courses, tying together walls made mainly of flint and stone. Smaller bricks used for floors have been found in many excavated Roman sites and can still be seen at the Roman Palace in Fishbourne.

When the Romans left Britain in 410AD, Saxon settlers took over and dwellings were once again constructed of timber, which was plentiful in Sussex. For 1,000 years no more bricks were produced in this part of the country. Their re-introduction, in the second half of the thirteenth century, was largely due to the founding of monastic and religious houses whose mother homes were in France where brick and tile making had become well established. Two of the earliest recorded tileries in Sussex, where mostly roofing tiles were made, were on land at Battle Abbey and its estate at Alciston.

Bricks were also being imported from the Netherlands and

Bands of Roman bricks at Pevensey Castle

Herstmonceux Castle, one of the earliest brick buildings in England

Flanders, mostly through the port of Winchelsea. Many of the bricks were pink or yellow coloured, and bricks of this type may be seen at Michelham Priory, Upper Dicker, and Old Place at Icklesham.

Herstmonceux Castle, built by Sir Roger Fiennes in 1440 at a cost of £3,800, was one of the first, and finest, edifices to be made entirely of Sussex bricks. Of a distinctive warm red colour, they were produced locally on a site at nearby Pevensey marshes where their manufacture was supervised by three expert craftsmen from Marlines in Flanders.

At a lecture given to the Society of Antiquaries on the January 20, 1757, the Dean of Exeter, Dr Thomas Lyttleton, on the subject of post Roman brick buildings in England, said of the castle: 'The art of making bricks was carried to such perfection, though it should seem to be in its infancy, that this vast structure has stood the brunt of weather for above five centuries, and particularly the salt corroding vapours arising from the sea, to which it is greatly exposed, without suffering the least injury in any part of the walls, insomuch that hardly a single brick shows the least mark of decay.'

By the 16th century brick making was well under way, many tile kilns being utilised to burn bricks as well, although a few bricks were still being imported from the Netherlands through the port of Rye. The brickmaking industry grew alongside the Wealden iron industry, bricks being needed for lining the many iron furnaces, and one of their earliest recorded uses is at Robertsbridge.

With the increasing demand for bricks, itinerant brickmakers found it more commercially viable to settle in one place and establish permanent brickyards. Many of these were on waste land of poor quality with thin topsoil, so suitable brick earth was near the surface and wood to fire the kiln was generally in plentiful supply. The brickmaker would usually obtain a lease from the owner of the land, with permission to extract brick earth and erect a kiln, for which he paid a rent.

As coastal resorts, such as Brighton, began to develop in the mid- 18th century, demand for bricks rose, leading to an acute shortage of 'on-site' building materials, so brick kilns began appearing beside many areas of expansion. The wood used for firing kilns along the coastal regions had been the readily available brushwood and furze, which provided the fierce heat required. But as the market for bricks kept growing so supplies of suitable wood diminished, and alternatives had to be sought.

More expensive coal, brought in by sea, was the obvious choice. Stanmer House at Brighton was made from bricks fired in coal burning kilns. By 1792 brickmakers at Lewes and Dicker had gone over to coal.

Coastal fortifications, erected against French invasion in the late 18th century, drew on large quantities of bricks, stretching many brickyards to capacity. A string of seventy-five Martello Towers was built between 1805 and 1808 along the Kent and Sussex coasts, using an estimated 500,000 bricks each. Some bricks were brought in by barge from London and, during a period of feverish activity, at least six extra brickyards were built between Eastbourne and Winchelsea to help in the production of some thirty-two million bricks for the towers.

In 1784, to raise revenue for the French wars, a brick tax had been imposed at a rate of 2s 6d per thousand, and this continued to rise in stages until it reached a peak of 5s 10d in 1805. At first, a strong demand for bricks equalled large profits for the brick

Martello Tower number 60 at Pevensey Bay, now converted to residential use

19

makers, but as the threat of a French invasion disappeared, the inevitable slump occurred. The brick tax had to be paid when the bricks were in their pre-firing stage, so the brickmaker had to bear any losses for those which were later damaged or unsold. As the recession took hold many protested about the tax and in 1850 it was eventually repealed, but by this time many brickyards had been forced out of business.

In the main most brickyards in Sussex were small local industries set up where they were needed. A limited amount of building material was moved around by horse and cart although this proved uneconomical. Transport by water was a popular choice, but as the railways opened up bricks were needed in large quantities for cuttings, tunnels, stations, bridges and viaducts. It is said that some sixteen million bricks were used for Hastings Tunnel and Bo-Peep Tunnel at St. Leonards. Temporary brick kilns were set up beside many railway lines and any extra bricks were brought in by rail or sea.

From this, a new breed of brickworks began to grow adjacent to railways lines, utilising the rail network to send out materials and bring in coal and coke to fire the kilns, and station brickyards were established at Robertsbridge, Hailsham, Partridge Green, Sharpthorne, Plumpton, Elsted and Rogate. Later, steam waggons superseded rail trucks, taking the bricks direct from manufacturer to the site with the minimum of handling and therefore less breakages.

By the second half of the 19th century there was a boom in the building trade, but with so much cheap labour about and by utilising 'on the spot' kilns, Sussex brickmakers were slow to invest in the labour saving machinery which was beginning to appear in other parts of the country.

The pugmill was probably one of the first mechanical devices to be used for mixing clay, replacing hand mixing with spades or treading with bare feet. Basically it was a wooden drum into which the wet clay was fed. Inside, several blades, attached to a vertical shaft, were turned with the assistance of horse-power, the animal plodding around the circular pugmill. Once the clay was ground to the right consistency it was extruded from the base of the pugmill. Eventually horsepower was, in most cases, replaced by steam engines, although water power was in use at Brightling.

The clay was made brick-shaped with the use of wooden moulds. When they were turned out the bricks were placed in a kiln; some 24,000 would fit into a small kiln. The brick-built kilns were heated slowly, so as not to damage the bricks, until the temperature reached 1,000°C, which was maintained for forty-eight hours. After a cooling period the bricks were removed, the whole process taking about six days.

Brickmaking was, by its very nature, a seasonal occupation. The brick earth was dug in the autumn and left exposed to the elements to temper. Bricks were made in late spring after the dangers of damage by frost had passed.

In 1875 Henry Johnson opened what was then the most modern brickworks in Sussex at Keymer Junction, where 300 men were provided with continuous work all year round. He also owned a brickyard and pottery business at Ditchling Common and both works had drying sheds, steam powered machinery and coal fired kilns.

By the late 1890s there were some 175 brickworks in Sussex, most of them in the east of the county. This was the maximum number ever recorded and by the turn of the century, with the inevitable peaks and troughs of industry, the trend was for much larger, and therefore fewer, businesses.

During the two world wars most of the brickworks in Sussex closed because of the blackout regulations; the glow from lit kilns could have provided beacons for enemy aircraft.

In 1945 there was an overwhelming need for a building programme to repair the ravages of war. Fifty-one of the larger pre-war brickyards opened up, but workers were in short supply. By 1951 just 1,495 are recorded as working in the brickmaking industry, where the number of Sussex companies had dropped to thirty-four. By 1959 the numbers had fallen even further, to just twenty-eight, and bricks were now having to compete against other building materials such as breeze and concrete blocks which were increasingly used for internal walls and rendered surfaces. To survive, companies merged and amalgamated, pooling their resources and reducing their costs. The losers closed.

One of the survivors, The Sussex Hand Made Brick Ltd, at Fourteen Acre Lane, Guestling, has twenty staff and specialises in an extensive range of hand made bricks. Former managing director Colin Davies said: 'We couldn't compete, pricewise, against big companies that can turn out a million bricks, often using robots for most areas of brick production, even down to the packaging, but we held our own with our hand made bricks, offering a wide range of facial characteristics and colours'.

The company was established in 1896, and apart from being closed between 1929 and the early Thirties, and during the Second World War, it has continued to produce bricks right up to the present day. They were still being burnt in the two coal-fired circular down-draught kilns until 1981, but today there is a modern square ceramic fibre kiln and five pre-firing dryers which hold 5,600 bricks each.

The machinery might be updated but brick making methods have changed little over the years. Material for the bricks is dug out with motor scrapers or excavators from a large quarry adjacent to the brickworks. The sandy earth, of high quality Fairlight clay, containing virtually no stones, is of characteristic red colour. It is transported by dump trucks to a clay stockpile alongside the works.

An excavator digs out clay from the stockpile and deposits it in a void in the ground where it is puddled with water until the clay has a 26 per cent moisture content. The resultant workable mixture is loaded into a circular feeder for further mixing and then sent along a conveyor and through a pair of differential medium speed rolls with a gap setting of 2mm further preparing the clay for brickmaking.

One of the two Hudson Berry brickmaking machines presses the clay mixture through a die into three-brick sanded moulds, the wet or green bricks are demoulded by hand and placed on steel perforated pallets which in turn are placed on stillages.

Colin Davies explained further: 'The second Berry machine is used as a plug mill to extrude clay clots through a die on to a conveyor. Hand moulders take the clay clot, roll it in sand and throw the clot into a sand-lined wooden mould made from high quality timber which is straight grained and free from imperfections.'

The company has thousands of different sized moulds. 'The excess clay is

An old brick kiln at Sussex Hand Made Bricks' yard at Guestling

cut off from the top of the mould with a bow wire, the mould is tapped lightly on diagonal corners and the brick is demoulded onto small brick sized wooden boards,' said Mr Davies.

The hand moulder places a wooden board on top of the brick and lifts the brick between the boards to place it on the edge of a steel perforated pallet. The system increases the number of bricks per pallet and reduces drying time.

Examples of special bricks made at Sussex Hand Made Bricks Ltd

The stillages are conveyed to the drying chambers, twenty-eight per dryer (5,600 bricks) where they are left for two days in a temperature of 80°C to reduce the moisture from twenty-six per cent to approximately two per cent. The bricks are now some five per cent smaller and hand set into packs of 604 or 704, depending upon the setting pattern required.

A multi-tined forklift sets the 54,000 bricks into the rectangular down-draught Propane heated kiln. Here they are left a further forty-four hours to fire in a temperature of 1,050°C, which gives the bricks an even, dark colour and makes them more frost resistant. They have now shrunk a further two per cent.

The heat given off by the cooling process (two to three days) is used to dry the bricks. The fired bricks are drawn with a multi-tined forklift and hand packed into 430 packs banded and shrink wrapped. They are then transported to numbered bays in the stockyard to await customers.

By specialising the company survives in an industry which may well be overproductive. Sussex brickmakers, no doubt, will continue to try and cope with the variable demands for their products in a fluctuating market. Sadly many businesses have long since vanished, leaving only names such as Brick Kiln Field or Kiln Cottages for posterity.

5

SUSSEX SHEPHERDS' CROOKS

A shepherd's crook was more than a practical tool of work, it was also a badge of office. The hooked end, or guide, was hand-made, generally of wrought iron, and was used to hook around the leg of an adult sheep or the neck of a lamb and so aid in its capture. Crooks fashioned from sections of gun barrels were considered the finest, and a limited number of brass ones were produced from a Brighton forge. But these tended to snap easily, so as curios are now regarded as collectors' items. Many superstitious shepherds never polished the metal ends, believing that they would attract lightning from thunderstorms passing over the Downs.

The long handle, known as a crook-stick, was made of hazel, ground-ash, cherry or straight holly. As metal crooks outlasted their wooden staffs a shepherd would have to smartly knock off the crook and fit a new stick which had been carved to fit.

Sometimes shepherds had 'best' crooks which were brought out on special occasions. Those in daily use were chosen to suit individual tastes; not too long or short, nor too heavy or light, they had to sit comfortably in the hand and become almost an extension of the user's arm.

At Pyecombe Forge some of the finest shepherds' crooks – the famous Pyecombe hooks – were made by a smith named Berry. Their manufacture was a well kept secret, the metal being tough enough and the hook, long, fine and curved enough so that even the most difficult sheep could be comfortably restrained. In the 1920s a Pyecombe hook cost the equivalent of 25p.

In later years, at the same forge, the tradition of producing fine crooks was carried on by iron worker Charles Mitchell. He had come to Sussex as a boy

An old time shepherd and his flock at a Downland dew pond

and was at Pyecombe for more than seventy years. His fine work was exported all over the world and one special crook won him a diploma at the Paris Exhibition of 1937. The Bishops of Chichester, Lewes, Croydon, Zululand and Uganda bought his Pyecombe hooks for use as pastoral staffs. When he died at the age of ninety-seven in 1942, at his funeral it seemed fitting that his son, George William Mitchell, carried the last crook his father had made two years earlier.

Other forges known for their high level of craftsmanship were at Falmer and Kingston-by-Lewes. A crook-maker named Green, at the Falmer forge, had a reputation both for the excellence of his workmanship and the uncertainty of his temper. A feature of his iron crooks was the fine curl at the end, produced with the help of a home-made iron curler.

At Kingston-by-Lewes, Phillip Hoather made crooks similar in style to the Pyecombe hook for fifty-seven years.

Dick Fowler, a Downland shepherd from East Dean, was rightly proud of his crook. It had served him well as he cared for his flock of Southdown sheep grazing between Belle Tout lighthouse and Michel Dean. On a June evening in 1929, as he walked home after folding (penning) his sheep for the night, he passed East Dean church where a confirmation

Tool used at Falmer Forge for crook-making

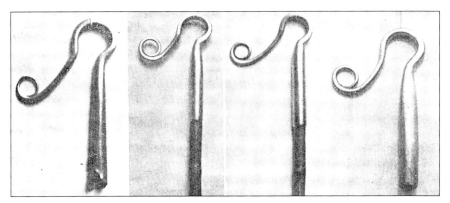

From the left: a crook of the famous old Pyecombe pattern; a crook made by Green of Falmer; a crook made by Hoather of Kingston-by-Lewes; the first brass crook made in Sussex

was being held. But the Bishop, Dr Walter Andrews, had forgotten his crozier, to the disappointment of the children awaiting confirmation. So, for the ceremony, this Sussex shepherd handed over his precious crook to another shepherd and, it is said, after that occasion, Dick looked at his crook with a new reverence and when he died in 1940 his crook was presented to the church in memory of the unusual incident.

Charles Mitchell at Pyecombe Forge

26

6

GRAY-NICOLLS CRICKET BATS

A perfect summer's day. The village green, a cricket team, the sound of leather on willow. Chances are that many of the cricket bats used around the county were made by the Gray-Nicolls company from the little Sussex village of Robertsbridge.

The famous cricketer WG Grace scored his hundredth century using a Gray-Nicolls bat. He wrote to the firm on October 8, 1895, saying: 'I used one of your bats in Hastings in 1894 and I scored 131. I may mention it was perfectly new. I kept it until this year and have scored over 2,000 runs with it. I used it when I made my 100th century and scored 1,000 runs in May with it. So I think I may call it my record bat. This year at Hastings I scored 104 runs with another of your bats and hope it will turn out as well as the old one.'

The company, originally known as LJ Nicolls, was founded in the 1870s by Levi Nicolls. He was by profession a carpenter and also a keen cricketer. As a hobby he made himself a cricket bat. It was so good that friends began asking him to produce more for them and the rest, as they say, is history.

Within a short time Levi Nicolls' white-willow hand-made cricket bats had gained a world-wide reputation for excellence and were used by many leading players. Levi experimented with different types of bats – one had the handle inclined strongly backwards, another had a wave-shaped rubber spring in the handle.

When he retired the business was managed by Percy Bridger, his son-in-law, and on *his* retirement in 1926, control passed to D Nicolls Bridger, Levi's grandson, and amateur Sussex cricketer AL Newbery. In 1940, under the concentration

WG Grace at the crease

of companies scheme, LJ Nicolls amalgamated with HJ Gray and Sons of Cambridge, which had previously acquired the bat-making company of Shaw and Shrewsbury Sports of Nottingham.

Gray, established in 1855, had a long history in racquet sports. A number of family members were leading racquet players. By the late nineteenth century the company had diversified into making other items of sporting equipment such as hockey sticks, golf clubs and cricket bats. Under the management of Horace George Gray, aided by his son, Harold, the company developed from a small family business into a thriving limited company. Amalgamation with Nicolls was a sound business venture as a wide range of sporting equipment could now be sold to players. And sell them they did. World class cricketers Ted Dexter, Richie Benaud, Alec Bedser and Frank Worrell were all using and endorsing Gray-Nicolls bats, as did all the captains of the Test-playing nations.

In the 1930s the partners, together with the company foreman, visited local Sussex woodlands each autumn to buy the willow. The wood had to be chosen carefully as had the ground in which it was growing. Fine blue-clay subsoil produced fine trees, but earth tainted with iron deposits produced unsuitable wood of a blackish hue. Trees aged between nine and twenty were selected and cut as close to the ground as possible, as the best wood was to be found nearest to the roots. The trunks were sawn on the spot into rough bat lengths and split into segments known as clefts.

Back at the workshop the clefts were trimmed with a circular saw until there was a hint of a bat shape. Afterwards they were seasoned outside for six months, with another half year under cover before being finished. Much of the work was done by hand.

The methods used today to complete the bats has changed little over the years. They have to go through seventy different stages, and when finished be able to perform at the highest level, withstanding the impact of a cricket ball travelling at seventy-five miles an hour or more.

Gray-Nicolls was responsible in the early 1970s for producing a fractionally lighter scoop-back bat, the GN100, where routed grooves in the back enabled the blade to be made wider, the edges thicker, increasing the overall size of the 'sweet spot' area where the bat hits the ball.

Over the years the company has developed other models, including the Scoop 200 and Dynadrive, using this same technology.

A Gray-Nicolls factory has now been set up in Melbourne, Australia. (See also Appendix 1 on page 105).

7

HARMER'S PLAQUES

Jonathan Harmer Jnr (1762-1849) was a talented stonemason and sculptor who lived in Heathfield. He was the son of Jonathan Harmer, also a stonemason, who on his death at the beginning of 1800, bequeathed to his two sons 'all such Portland and other stone, together with my working tools and utensils belonging to the trade of stone mason, brick layer and land surveying books'.

An example of Harmer's terracotta work at Anne of Cleves House Museum

As an ardent Republican young Jonathan Harmer emigrated to the United States in 1796 to join his brother John, who had sailed some two years previously, but when his father died he returned to take over the family business, which he ran until 1839.

Times were hard at the beginning of the nineteenth century and he took pity on those whose slim finances would stretch only to the cost of a simple headstone. He began to fashion ornamental bas-relief terracotta memorial plaques from the local red clay which he often combined with paler imported clay. These plaques could then be affixed at a later time. To help keep costs down he made his own clay moulds and thus could turn out a number of identical panels instead of carving each one individually.

Two matching plaques showing a basket of flowers and fruit are on headstones in Warbleton (John Fox, died 1815) and Glynde (Marianne New, died 1811, aged ten).

An angel plaque on display in the same museum

Many were fashioned in the same image as he carved in marble – cherubs, urns of flowers and angels. Or customers could choose their own designs. Surviving examples of his terracotta work can be seen at the Anne of Cleves House Museum in Lewes. They are a cherub with crown and rays; plaques representing crowns; pateras of flowers; a plaque representing an angel; a small urn with mould; a group representing Charity; a Masonic tablet representing Faith and Hope; a basket of fruit and flowers.

The plaques were a great success and Jonathan's sons joined the business, although one, Sylvan, pursued the occupation of land surveyor.

Some of Jonathan Harmer's work can still be seen in Sussex churchyards, including those at Hailsham, Cade Street, Chiddingly, Mayfield,

A Harmer plaque on a tomb in Hailsham churchyard

Hastings, Salehurst, Heathfield, Burwash and Framfield. Other plaques may be seen in Brighton Museum.

In Wartling churchyard is probably the only example of Jonathan Harmer's work cast in iron, that of a basket of flowers and fruit. It may well have been made at Ashburnham furnace, at that time the only one working in East Sussex.

Jonathan Harmer died in 1849, aged eighty-six and he was buried in Heathfield churchyard on February 2, 1849.

8

MINTS

In the tenth and eleventh centuries it was the custom for the king to grant selected towns the right to mint coins. These were mainly silver pennies and half-pennies, although there was the occasional striking of special gold coins. At that time Sussex had six mints, each paying a royalty for the privilege of using officially approved dies. Before that time Sussex coinage had been supplied either by a travelling mint or from minting places in Lewes and Chichester.

King Edgar on a silver penny

The English royal coinage attained its finest development under Edgar, who reigned from 959 to 975. His coinage was uniform throughout the realm and used as a model during the next two centuries. Edgar's penny bore both the name of the mint and the moneyer who issued it.

PEVENSEY

The site of the Old Mint House, Pevensey, has a fascinating history. Here, in 1076, during the reign of William the Conqueror, stood a Norman mint (or mynte) mentioned in the Domesday Book, where workmen were engaged in striking coins for the first Norman King of England.

King Stephen on a silver penny, 1146

The mint is opposite the eastern postern of Pevensey Castle. Over the years there has been much speculation as to why the mint had not been incorporated within the castle walls. Pevensey Castle at that time was a neglected Roman fortress, with little left standing apart from a circle of massive walls.

William had given it to his half brother, Count Robert of Mortain who, in 1069, began to build a moated Norman castle on the site. But its erection was slow. The mint, unable to be accommodated in the castle had, instead, to be located nearby and it is noted in the Domesday Book that a rent of

The Old Mint House, Pevensey, now an antiques shop

twenty shillings a year was paid to the Earl of Mortain. There are stories that suggest a tunnel was built between the Mint House and the Castle keep.

Coins were minted here not only for William, but also for William Rufus (by a moneyer named as AElfheh), Henry I and King Stephen (moneyers Alwine and Felipe). Operations appear to have ceased soon after the accession of Henry II in 1154.

Within the present building, which dates back to 1342, there are traces of the original minting chamber but the coiners' furnaces have long vanished. Some of the coins struck at this Sussex Mint, inscribed PEFNESE are on display in provincial museums and in the British Museum.

CHICHESTER

This town appears to have been one of the first to have received the right to establish a mint in 928 under a new law for the regulation of coinage. In 1204 three dies were made, two for the King, one for the Bishop.

In 1208 all those working at the mint were ordered to take the sealed dies to Westminster and await directions from the king. History, unfortunately, does not appear to have recorded the reasons.The mint name on the coins varied, but included CICES, CICHI, CISSAN and CIV.

HASTINGS

Under the same law as applied at Chichester, Hastings had one permitted mint, originally situated in a wooden castle that was later rebuilt of stone by William the Conqueror. It had a prolific output, second only to Lewes. Mint names here included HASTIEN, HSTI, HASTING and AE

LEWES

This town's mint was considered to be the most important in Sussex and was granted two moneyers. It is recorded in the Domesday Book that in the reign of Edward the Confessor they each had to pay twenty shillings (two thirds to the king, one third to the landowner, Earl Warrene) each time the money was renewed. Mint names on coins included LEWEII, LEW and LAE.

RYE

This was a small mint with one moneyer, named Rawulf, which was established during the reign of Stephen. The inscription is RYE.

STEYNING

This mint, although a one-moneyer establishment, issued large numbers of coins during the reigns of Canute, Harold I, Harthacnut, Edward the Confessor, Harold II and William I and II, and appears to have ceased production in 1100. The mint name was STING, STENC or STAE.

9

SMOCKS

Sussex smocks, or round-frocks, were a favoured traditional garment of the farming and rural fraternity during the seventeenth and early eighteenth centuries. They were loose fitting, deep pocketed, all-purpose garments made of coarse calico, many decorated with distinctive honeycomb needlework on the yoke and shoulders. Designed without a front opening, and weatherproofed with linseed oil, they could be worn either way over corduroy trousers and removed by being pulled up over the head.

A similar, but shorter garment, with buttons down the front was known as a Banyan. Adapted from an Indian design, this was worn for fair-weather manual work. Round-frocks were used during inclement weather to protect more of the body, although a fleecy-lined great coat or a canvas cape proofed with oil or pitch was worn on the top during severe conditions.

White smocks made of fine material and embellished with ornamental needlework were donned for special occasions such as weddings, funerals, Sundays and holidays. Black or grey ones were worn during the working week and green ones for shooting parties. A prospective farmer's wife needed to be able to make a round frock and 'a Beef staak puddun' for her husband. An embroidered smock-frock was often the first gift from wife to husband after marriage.

From the Brede Poor Book of 1759:

Paid to Mary Inkpen for making of a round-frock for J. Colget...8d.
Paid for making a round-frock to Dame Inkpen for Jas. Hockum....7d.

'Old Tom' in his voluminous smock

To Widow Inkpen for macking of John Brattels Frock..........6d.

William Cobbett, writing in *Rural Rides*, stated that when he got to Horsham many men and boys were wearing round-frocks, more than he had seen in any other county. And in a 1927 edition of the *Sussex County Magazine* a reader, Caleb Thornton, wrote that during the First World War, when he was working at the Cliffe Foundry, Lewes, his work took him weekly to the cattle market 'and I was very much surprised to see that the round-frock was still being worn by Lewes men'.

Browne and Crosskey, on the Eastgate Street-High Street corner in Lewes, made Sussex smocks in a limited variety of colours for more than a hundred years. Apart from the usual khaki and biscuit, black, grey or dark blue were favoured by shepherds, drab by cowmen, royal blue by butchers.

John Arnall (in 1845), foreman at Colbrans Farm, Laughton, in round frock, beaver hat and gaiters

Frank Upton, who had been a shepherd at West Blatchington Farm for fifty years from 1883, recounted to writer Barclay Wills that the Lewes Sheep Fair held on the September 21 each year was regarded as not only a fair day but a 'clothing day' as well.

Browne and Crosskey was besieged by shepherds who made for the outfitting department, which was at the top of a staircase. Big coats, crooks and dogs were left at the foot of the stairs, whilst assorted packing cases were put on the pavement outside to serve as seats for waiting wives and friends.

Once a customer asked for 'a hog stopper'. He found the smocks effective for helping to capture awkward swine. By crouching in front of the animal the voluminous material provided a perfect trap for a pig in forward motion.

By the late 1800s the smock had fallen out of favour, ousted by the shirt and jacket. Although still common during the First World War, it had virtually disappeared by the Second.

In the 1970s and 1980s Julian Akers-Douglas ran a modern smock-making business in East Hoathly. She employed skilled local needlewomen and, using the best natural fabrics, was able to produce a range of traditional and highly contemporary clothing. Each was a one-off original and many included Julian's own unique embroidery design which she named Barham Smock, after the hamlet where she lived. The new-style Sussex smocks proved very popular and sold all around the world.

A Julian Akers-Douglas design

10

SELSEY MOUSE TRAPS

Colin Pullinger, from the Isle of Seals, Selsey, near Chichester, was a businessman with considerable inventive talents, the Clive Sinclair of his day. His trade card stated that he was a contractor, inventor, fisherman and mechanic and that he followed 'the various trades of a Builder, Carpenter, Joiner, Sawyer, Undertaker, Turner, Cooper, Painter, Glazier, Wood Pump Maker, Paper Hanger, Bell Hanger, Sign Painter, Boat Builder'.

Furthermore, he was a clock cleaner, repairer of clocks, and fitter keys; he repaired umbrellas and parasols; mended china and glass; was a copying clerk, letter writer, accountant and teacher of navigation.

The card went on to list Pullinger's other business interests and skills, among them grocer, baker and farmer, assessor and collector of taxes, surveyor, house agent, land measurer, assistant overseer, seaman, ship's cook, steward, mate and navigator, and clerk to the parish, to the police and to Selsey Sparrow Club.

Among his inventions were an improved horseshoe, an improved scarifier, a grass rake, a machine to tar ropes, an improved velocipede and a 'Vessel to Cut-Asunder Chains put across the mouth of the harbour'.

Pullinger is probably best remembered for his mouse trap. This, he said, was 'made on a scientific Principle, where each one caught resets the Trap to catch its next neighbour. Requires no fresh baiting and will catch them by the dozens'. The trap, he claimed would never wear out. As well as selling his mouse traps, he hired them out.

Born at Ivy Cottage, High Street, Selsey, in 1815, the son of a carpenter, Pullinger went to sea as a youth, but having sailed through some terrible storms which 'made a deep impression on me and led me to reflect seriously on life', he decided to use 'the talents with which Providence had entrusted me, an inventive mind'.

From his Inventive Factory, which employed more than forty people, he turned out some 960 fourteen-inch long 'Curious Mouse Traps' each week, which sold for half a crown. So popular were they that they were carried by cart to Chichester to be sent all over the world. There was even an extraordinary story that several wealthy local people got together to build the old Selsey light railway to transport the mousetraps.

The mice, tempted by a bait of wheat, would enter by a hole in the side and

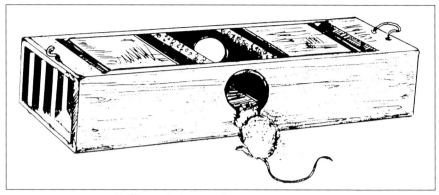

Pullinger's famous humane mouse trap

be tipped by a see-saw trap into one of the end chambers (capable of holding six or more captives), causing the apparatus to re-set automatically. The rodents were not killed and could be released away from habitation through a tin slide in the bottom. At the Great Exhibition of 1851, in the Crystal Palace, London, Pullinger mousetraps were displayed for an audience which included Queen Victoria.

When Colin Pullinger died in 1889 his son, Charles, and the workforce, carried on the business, but it began to dwindle away in the face of competition from the 'penny traps'. In the end, only Charles remained, working from a tiny, dilapidated white building, finding just enough business to keep producing these special beechwood mouse traps. With his bowler hat worn at a jaunty angle, he could, once the materials were prepared, take just three minutes to assemble each trap.

The business ceased trading in the early 1920s when Charles Pullinger retired.

Charles Pullinger at work

38

11

TRUGS

Willow, willow, bend it true,
Here's a Sussex trug for you.
First the chestnut frame you form,
Steam it gently, soft and warm,
Then bend it round the pattern mould
And drive in nails, firm and bold.
Then the willow smooth and white,
Into the frame fit snug and tight.
A Sussex trug is strong and good
Though light in weight the willow wood.

Sussex trugs are known throughout the world but today are commercially produced in just one small area of Sussex at Herstmonceux. Many gardeners favour these versatile slatted wooden baskets for pick-and-carry jobs because they are durable and strong. So tough in fact, it is said that they can, when upended, be sat upon. With care, a trug can last fifty or sixty years. What makes Sussex trugs unique in these days of mass production is that, four hundred years on, they are still being made in the same traditional fashion using local woods of sweet chestnut and willow.

The name trug is derived from the Anglo-Saxon word trog, meaning a trough or boat-shaped wooden vessel. In spite of the antiquity of the name, these baskets, as we know them today, appeared in the early 15th century and were defined in a dictionary published in 1670, as an old local measure for wheat, equal to two thirds of a bushel.

A signboard displayed outside the shop of cooper David Wratten, 59 High Street, Hailsham, in the 1870s, bore the following words:

As other people have a sign,
I say just stop and look at mine.
Here Wratten, cooper, lives and makes
Ox bows, trug baskets and hay rakes.

Sells shovels both for flour and corn,
And shauls and makes a good box churn.

Around the 1820s, Thomas Smith, a native of the village of Herstmonceux, is recognised as having developed the trugs familiar to us today. From the round coracle shape long favoured by farmers for grain measures or animal feed balers, he found that by adding small feet and handles, they were ideal containers for carrying cut flowers and plants, harvesting garden vegetables and were even strong enough to carry logs.

Around 1829, Smith began the first commercial production of his trugs or trucks. Over the years he displayed his wares at many exhibitions, including the Universal Exhibition in Paris of 1855 and the Fisheries Exhibition at Edinburgh in 1884. At the Great Exhibition of 1851 in the Crystal Palace in London, he won a gold medal, an Order of Merit and an order from Queen Victoria.

The Queen admired the baskets and ordered a consignment for the royal gardens. It is said that Thomas Smith made them all himself, decorated them with silver nails, then piled them into a handcart and pushed it the sixty miles to London to deliver them personally, not wanting to trust anyone else with such responsibility. His enterprise earned him a Royal Warrant.

The business flourished and became known as Royal Sussex Trugs. As demand grew for Sussex trugs some twenty-four satellite workshops started

Large trug in use as a log basket

40

up in the area – at Cowbeech, Windmill Hill and East Hoathly, and R Reed and Son, a rival manufacturer, started in Herstmonceux.

This was Reuben A Reed (1848-1927), a gifted local trug maker who, in 1899, moved into a cottage now known as The Truggery, where he and his son Thomas (1878-1946) lived a spartan life. Thomas was taught the art of trug making by expert Ben Catt, who lived a couple of miles away in Cowbeech. A good trug maker can turn out some fifty baskets a week; it takes a year to be reasonably competent, two years to become proficient.

Rupert Reed, Thomas's son, made trug baskets all his working life and his three sisters, Dora, Pamela and Mollie, helped run the business. When Mollie was born her father made her a special cradle. It was a large trug without a handle, fitted instead with rockers.

She recalled helping to run the family shop, which also sold a variety of other goods from bicycles, Dicker pottery and tyres to petrol in two gallon cans. Mollie said that in the 1930s the Reeds put up a large shed in nearby Plat Field to house timber, a sawbench and planer run by a petrol engine. It was her job to keep the place tidy and remove the sawn boards as Rupert finished with them.

From early in the 19th century there was a lucrative American trade. Container loads of trugs, mostly number 6 (20inx12in) were shipped out to California, at a cost of 2/9d each. These were special hand-cleft clinker or clincher-built baskets which cost an extra threepence. Much of that business was lost after the Wall Street crash of 1929.

In the 1930s a company in France placed regular bulk orders for small painted trugs which they then filled with artificial flowers and sold on.

Thomas Reed used often to rise at 4am to tie together bundles of trugs ready to send out all over Britain. Isteds, the local carrier, would transport them to Hailsham railway station. Here they were stored with no visible consignee addresses because rival firms were always eager to find out more about Reed's wholesale contacts and trade prices.

The trug companies of R Reed and Son and Royal Sussex Trugs were brought together by marriage when Thomas's sister-in-law, Muriel married Edward C Smith in 1923. But the two firms, arch rivals right up to the present day, still traded separately.

Trug baskets were originally constructed from local woods, the frames made of sweet chestnut, as it felt smooth to a lady's hand, combined with overlapping slats of willow which formed the body.

Buying suitable wood was, and is, a capricious exercise. Many purchases of this cash crop are heavily dependent upon networking for supplies which need to be bought one or two years in advance to allow it to season.

Supplies of sweet chestnut are still bought locally from coppiced woodlands. About seven feet is cut from the butt end which gives the trugs their strength. The wood is split with a special cleaving axe and left to season for about six months. The outer strips, with the bark intact, are used for the handles and rims, shaped by being steamed in a copper steamer (fired by the waste wood), for about fifteen to twenty minutes, then bent around wooden formers.

Willow needs to be straight-grained and free from knots. Some supplies have come from the cricket bat manufacturer, Grey Nicholls of Robertsbridge, which uses only the finest quality willow. Alternative stocks may come in the shape of whole trees from either local plantations, or Essex and East Anglia.

The trunks are quartered, peeled and left out to season. When ready they are cut into thin boards, shaved smooth and, with the aid of an ingenious wooden contrivance called a dolly or shaving horse, shaped and curved with a draw knife. Dunked in water, the boards become pliable enough to nail into place. Five or seven overlapping strips form the main body of the basket.

Inside The Truggery at Herstmonceux

At The Truggery there are about 100 variations of trugs, both plain and fancy. The eleven rectangular sizes are ideal for harvesting garden produce, weeding, carrying pot plants or collecting eggs. Long stemmed flowers will fit comfortably into the 23inx12in shallow based trug, and the elongated cucumber basket has two handles for balance. There is a walking stick trug, where a stick is incorporated into the body of the basket, useful for those who are

Mollie Reed

arthritic and have difficulty bending down. This was developed at the end of the last century for women to carry their work (sewing etc) into the garden.

Customers from all over the world buy trugs and most are still used in the garden, while others become bread baskets or bathroom towel holders. A trug has been used to rescue a kitten that had tumbled down a deep well. The creature was given up for lost but three days later it was heard crying. Buckets and baskets lowered on ropes failed to get it out, until a trug was let down containing some pieces of rabbit and a saucer of milk. The hungry cat stepped into the trug and was quickly drawn up.

Queen Elizabeth the Queen Mother has a collection of decorated square trugs, supplied when she was the Duchess of York, and a note on the wall of The Truggery states that two of the size 0 (7fiinx3in) were supplied to her daughters, the Princesses Elizabeth and Margaret Rose.

Mollie Reed remembered the occasion. 'One Sunday morning in the 1930s a lady knocked at the door of the shop wanting to buy two small hand painted trugs. Because it was a Sunday my mother did not want to sell them. The lady pointed to a stationary car along the road and said that she was nanny to the little princesses, and they wanted the trugs to play with on Cooden beach. So my mother succumbed and a sale was made.'

In 1978 The Reeds sold The Truggery to former ceramic teacher David Sherwood and his wife Sue, who owned RW Rich and Sons, maker of wooden

agricultural implements, of East Hoathly. The couple took on six full and part-time employees and business boomed.

The firm changed hands again in 1994 when it was bought by Sarah Page and her husband Mark, a commercial pilot, who had been looking for a business selling hand crafted items. Mark, who had been a fencer and gatemaker, knew about wood but, Sarah said, they had to learn as they went along. Another problem was finding skilled workers. 'There was someone using the workshop when we bought The Truggery and we asked him if he would like to stay on and help us and one of the previous trug makers came back.'

One employee, Tim Franks, has been a trug maker since 1989. Having liked woodwork at school he went on to do a one year carpentry course and was then taught trug making at The Truggery. He works in tandem with Pete Marsden who has always been interested in coppiced country crafts and was trained at Merristwood College, Guildford.

As recently as 1945 there were some twenty-four small local companies making trugs, but today, apart from a handful of one-man-band trug makers working from home, there are now just two commercial premises left, Thomas Smith's Trug Shop and The Truggery.

In spite of growing competition from cheaper, factory made, plywood and plastic ones, Sussex trugs continue to sell at both Herstmonceux businesses, proof indeed that discerning people will always pay for long lasting, quality baskets turned out by skilled craftsmen in the heart of Sussex. (See also Appendix 2 illustrating an early 20th century price list for trug baskets).

12

THE BRIGHTON BUBBLE CAR

In 1957 it cost £399, weighed 360kg and achieved around 70mpg, pushed along by a 250cc single-cylinder motorcycle engine. The Isetta bubble car, with its front opening door, was originally produced by the Italian firm of ISO Spa, which made refrigerators, scooters, motorcycles and three-wheeled vans at works near Milan.

An Italian engineer named Preti presented an innovative design of a small, two-person town car to Renzo and Pero Rivolta of ISO Spa and at the 1953 Turin Motor Show the teardrop-shaped Isetta (little ISO) was launched.

Franchise rights of production were sold to several companies, including BMW. The production of British-made Isettas, built under licence from BMW in Germany, was the brainchild of former BOAC pilot, RJ Ashley, who gave up his job as director and general manager of Armstrong-Sidley at Coventry to work on the Isetta project.

The Isetta, made in Brighton

The first British-made Isettas came off the production line on April 23, 1957 and were welcomed by many as an effective answer to the rising price and shortage of petrol. They were assembled in the decommissioned main engine shed of Brighton Locomotive Works, which had a railway line running through the middle. Many of the workforce had previously been employed here, assembling or repairing 70-ton railway engines; now they had to adapt to 7cwt vehicles.

Each Saturday morning a trainload of assorted parts to make some 250 cars arrived from BMW in Germany (engine, gearbox and, for early cars, body panels). The chassis was made by Rubery-Owen in the Midlands, and other parts were supplied by Lucas Electrics and Girling Brakes. From Monday to Friday freight trains took completed cars to London from where they were forwarded all over Britain.

'This is a car for someone seeking transport rather than sport, whose aim is economy rather than luxury, but who is prepared to sacrifice nothing in terms of reliability,' said a review in T*he Motor Cycle* on December 29, 1960.

The clutch pedal appeared to be superfluous once first gear had been engaged. A turn of the key and the car would be off. With a length of 7ft 9in (2.36m) parking was easy.

Although the first Isettas were four-wheelers, a number of three-wheelers were made to take advantage of the UK's cheaper motorcycle licence, which covered this design. The production line was moved to Victoria Road, Portslade, in 1961, where the vehicles were made until 1964.

13

GLASS MAKING

As for glassmakers, they be scant in the land,
Yet one there is, as I do understand.
And in Sussex is now his habituation,
At Chiddingfold he works of his occupation.
WD Scull, from *Breviary of Philosophy*,
by Thomas Charnock, 1557

The Wealden glass industry, in many respects, seems to have been overshadowed by the more important and certainly more widespread iron industry. Glass making was active for four centuries around Kirdford and Wisborough Green in north-west Sussex, although the most productive area in the England was just over the border, at Chiddingfold in Surrey. For glass manufacture, as for iron, wood was an essential item. Here again the great forests of the Weald were plundered to provide charcoal for the furnaces.

Glass making appears to have originated from Syria and Egypt in about 4000 BC and spread to Phoenicia, then Rome, Spain, Gaul and Germany. The basic composition of glass has changed little from earliest times. It consists roughly of about seventy-five per cent silica (usually sand), ten per cent lime (soda ash), and fifteen per cent sodium or potassium oxide, the flux to facilitate melting. Its manufacture was such an intricate and closely guarded secret that glassmaking families often intermarried.

Although glassware, goblets, bottles, glazed beads, mirrors and mosaics had been imported from Gaul for some considerable time, there is speculation that the art of glass-making may have come to England with the Roman invasion in 43AD. Equally, there is strong argument that French and Dutch settlers may have brought their glass-making skills with them, travelling from the flourishing glass industry areas of Lorraine and Normandy to Littlehampton and, via the Arun, to take up residence in and around Wisborough Green, Loxwood, Plaistow and Kirdford, areas of the Weald rich in the necessary sands, trees and water.

Evidence of early manufacture of glass in the Weald is scant. In 675 Benedict Biscop sent messengers to France to fetch glass-makers to glaze the windows, side chapels and clerestory of his church, and not only did they finish the work that was required of them, but also taught their craft.

By the 13th century glassmaking had became well established at Chiddingfold and Pickhurst, north of Petworth. Here, around 1240, a settler from Normandy, Laurence Vitrearius de Dunkshurstlonde, was making window glass on a twenty acre plot of land known as Dyers Cross, for both Westminster Abbey and Salisbury Cathedral. He is the first glassmaker to be named in historical records.

The Chiddingfold glass tradition seems to have then been carried on by John le Alemayne who, between 1350 and 1356, provided window glass for St Stephen's Chapel, Westminster Palace, for a total cost of £240, and Richard Holmere who, in 1352, provided white and imported azure glass for the Chapter House, Westminster. Both also acted as dealers (Holmere had a depot at Candlewick Street in the City of London) and travelled around the country selling 'cuppis to drinck with, urynalls, bottles, bowles, and such lyke'.

Another French glass-making family, the Schurterres, arrived at Chiddingfold in 1343. A quarter of a century later John Schurterre, now an established landowner, bought John le Alemayne's business at nearby Frome, to add to his two Chiddingfold works and furnace at Strudwick Wood, Kirdford. On his death in 1379, his widow Joan put in a manager from Staffordshire, John Glazewryth, to supervise the business for six years until her young son came of age.

Much of the output here was of window glass, tableware being of secondary importance. With the expiry of his contract in 1386, John Glazewryth set himself up with his own glass furnace in the Chiddingfold area. This he later sold to a Henry Ropley, a glass carrier.

By the 15th century the Peytowes (Peytos) family were the big name in glass-making, holding virtually a local monopoly and owning most of the furnaces in the district and about 1,500 acres of woodland which was, in part, providing much-needed fuel for their glasshouses.

Saxon horn glass

A century later the glass industry was having to compete with the iron industry for depleting timber supplies and even the waters from the streams. Imported German, Venetian and Dutch glass was making inroads into the Wealden glass industry. Chiddingfold started to lose its share of the market.

Around this time Jean Carre, a Flemish glassmaker living in London, saw the opportunity of cornering the English market. He had leant his craft in Antwerp, and decided to bring over a number of refugee Huguenots from Lorraine and Normandy to work in his Sussex glasshouses at Wisborough Green. With them came the Hensey, or Hennezels, brothers, who bought a fifty per cent share of the Carre company and negotiated a generous contract that not only paid them wages as skilled workmen but half the net profits as well.

Many of the Huguenot glassmakers integrated themselves into English society and found financial backing from the affluent land-owning local gentry. Such mutual agreements brought together the skilled French glassmakers and the wood they so badly needed.

To further promote his businesses at Wisborough Green, probably run by the Hensey brothers, Carre then petitioned Queen Elizabeth I, in 1567, for a licence. The licence (monopoly) he was after was to make vessel glass of Venetian style in London and window glass in the Weald to be run by the glassmakers he had introduced. This was refused, but he was given a twenty-one year licence on September 8, 1567, to make 'glas for glasinge such as is made in France, Burgundy and Lorraine'. This was granted on the condition that he and one of his other partners, Anthony Beku, submitted proper accounts, paid royalties, taught the art of glassmaking to a select number of Englishmen and build two new glass furnaces before Christmas 1568. By this time stocks of suitable wood were becoming scarce. For these furnaces Carre appears to have bought timber from woods around Arundel, shipping it by barge up the Arun.

Inscribed Saxon bottle

Shortly afterwards, the firm of Carre and Beku applied to Sir William Cecil for permission to cut wood and make charcoal in Windsor Great Park. If this was for their furnaces in Sussex, transport would have been expensive. As Windsor Castle was undergoing extensive structural alterations it might be assumed another glass furnace was to be set up nearby to provide on-the-spot glass for the windows.

In 1568 Carre invited three cousins of the Hensey brothers, Thomas and Balthazar Hensey and Jean Chevalier, to come to England from Vosges, in Lorraine, with 'four gentlemen glasiers' to build two ovens so 'they could every day make, in eche of the said oovens, the quantitie of thirtie bundelles of glas whyte or coullers good lawfull and merchauntable of good height and largnes well proportioned'.

Because Carre had effectively brought in more business partners, with a nine-year contract, without, apparently, telling Beku, their business relationship went sour. In July 1568 two of Carre's employees, Peter and John Bongar, attacked James Arnold, Beku's son-in-law, one with a heavy staff the

49

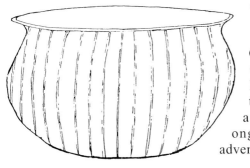

Saxon bowl in the Roman style

other with a hot iron rod. Arnold was wounded and badly burnt.

On August 11, 1569, a Special Commission appointed Richard Onslow and William More to listen to both parties involved in the affray and make an acceptable judgement, as the ongoing quarrel might have an adverse effect on the production of English glass. As Becku and his employees were found to be 'sober and honest men' the Bongars had to pay forty shillings damages to Arnold.

By early 1569 Carre's company owned three glass furnaces in the Wealden area and Carre had become an important man in this now rapidly expanding trade. In his London factory he began to make crystal glass and used some of the immigrant French glassmakers working at Wisborough Green furnace. However they were not experienced in its manufacture, so he brought over skilled Venetian workers, including a Jacob Verzelini, and in 1571 Carre's London factory, an abandoned monastery known as Crutched Friars, complete with new round furnace, was the first permanent establishment for making crystal glass in England.

He died just a year later and was buried at Alford on the May 25, 1572. In his will he bequeathed to his wife Jane Campe 'half the lease of the woods and of the grounds of Fernfold in Sussex, also also my movables and immovables for her life after my debts have been paid'.

Although Carre never lived to see the results of all his hard work, Jacob Verzelini (1522-1606), who had become his assistant, did. When the Crutched Friars factory burnt down, he moved to Broad Street where, in 1575, he was granted a royal patent 'for drinking and other glasses.' Penalties for infringement were ten shillings a glass and £200 per furnace.

When Carre's licence of twenty-one years came up for renewal in 1589 glassmaker George Longe, who had works in Ireland, applied for it, pointing out that Carre had not paid royalties, some glasshouses had been operating without licences, the art was not being taught to Englishmen, large areas of forest were being laid to waste and other conditions were not being fulfilled. Certainly one furnace at Sidney Wood, north of Loxwood, had been operated so discreetly by Carre that it would appear he wished to avoid paying royalties to Elizabeth I. However Longe's complaints did not appear to get him very far as Verzelini carried on successfully until 1592 when he passed the business monopoly patent on to Sir Jerome Bowes and retired.

Shipbuilding and the ordnance trade were making great inroads in the Wealden forests. The supply of wood was becoming critical, so much so that many of the immigrant glassmakers were being pushed out by the ironmasters who needed all the timber they could get for the production of much-needed ordnance. Guns were a necessity, glass a luxury. For those glassmakers who stayed things turned nasty when Lord Burleigh discovered, and managed to stop, a plot to rob, murder and burn down the houses of French glassmakers living around Petworth.

The anti-French feeling provoked a Bill in 1585 'against the making of glass by strangers and outlandish men within the realm and for the preservation of timber and woods spoiled by glasshouses'. It also stated that one Englishman had to be employed for every two foreigners and that no timber could be cut within twenty-two miles of London, seven miles of Guildford and four miles of Rye and Pevensey, or the foot of the hills 'called the Downs of Sussex'. The Bill failed to receive the Royal Assent. Disturbed by the depth of feeling against them, many glassmakers began moving westwards into Hampshire. The ironmasters, 'following the wood', took over.

In 1608, Albert Hensey, who was working one of the Wisborough Green furnaces, which was leased, for £3 a year, in the name of Isaack Bungar (aliens could not themselves take on a lease), returned from church to find that the yeoman landowner, Thomas Jackson, with many

Twisted Saxon ale cup

of his relatives armed 'with bows, arrows, pykes, staves and muskettes', had tried to break into the glasshouse. Two of Albert Hensey's servants had refused them entry, with the result Thomas Jackson broke in, beat up the servants and seized the stock.

Defending his actions, Thomas Jackson said he had never made a lease with Albert Hensey, only Isaack Bungar. Hensey had entered the building and refused to let anyone go near it and rent was owed. It seems that Bungar had been keeping the money Hensey had paid to him.

It is not clear why Isaac Bungar should have pocketed the money. A second generation Norman, his forbears came over to teach glassmaking to the English and prospered. Isaac had been described as 'a master and owner of glass furnaces in Surrey and Sussex'. He conducted services at Kirdford church. An ambitious man, he owned considerable tracts of woodland and was one of the Weald's chief glass producers. To aid in marketing his wares, he joined up with Lionel Bennett, a London glass dealer and a member of the Glazier's Company. Between them they managed to corner a large portion of the market, to the point that their customers complained they had monopolised all the glass made in Sussex. It was so scarce under their domination that they were forced to cast lots for the available supply and many could scarcely obtain enough glass to make a living for their families.

French glassmakers were still drifting away to areas where they were perhaps more welcome and supplies of wood more plentiful. But the Wealden glassmaking industry was dealt its final death blow when a James 1 Proclamation of 1615 prohibited the further use of wood 'in melting glass in any factory in England'. Coal would have to be used instead, which meant technical changes would have to be made to the furnaces.

A sixteenth century unguent bottle found on the site of a Wisborough Green furnace. Probably it was discarded because it was misshapen

Isaac Bungar, now wealthy and still ambitious, was not prepared to give up the old ways. He had many a head-on collision with Admiral Sir Robert Mansell, who had been granted a licence to make glass using new coal-fired furnaces at Verzelini's former Broad Street factory.

Isaac, it seems, was prepared to hire away Mansell's workmen or bribe others to spoil some of the batches of glass. Mansell eventually had to prosecute Bungar to close down his furnace, although he did try and hold out an olive branch by offering him £200 a year to oversee his new coal factories. Isaac refused and continued with his glassmaking. So Mansell successfully prosecuted him in the Court of Exchequer and although Isaac's wood-fired furnaces were forcibly closed down in 1618 he continued to be a thorn in Mansell's side by remaining in the retail trade as well as being active member of the Glaziers Company.

For four centuries, from an area of the Weald no more than ten miles square, came the greatest production of glass in England, especially during the 16th century. Today, apart from a few place names, there is little material or archaeological evidence remaining of the forty-two sites. (See Appendix 3)

14

WEALDEN IRON

Only the names survive today – Burnt Oak, Furnace Lane, Hammer Pond, Minepit Wood, Forge Farm. Apart from these there is now little evidence that the Weald of Sussex was, for two distinct historical periods, a thriving, noisy, iron-producing area, the 'black country' of England.

From Chithurst in the west to Brede in the east there were more than a hundred sites sandwiched between the North and South Downs. This area had (and still has) rich veins of iron ore, and there were once vast forests providing the almost unlimited fuel that was needed for making furnace charcoal, plus convenient waterways – the Arun, Adur, Ouse, Cuckmere, Rother and Medway rivers – for transport.

Iron technology reached Britain from Europe in around the first century BC via a Celtic tribe called the Brythons. By the time the Romans invaded Britain in AD43 the smelting of iron was an active, substantial and well established industry, especially around Rye and Hastings. Its potential was almost certainly recognised by Emperor Claudius and may well have influenced his desire to extend the Roman Empire to Britain. Many a Roman road was partly made from the waste slag and cinders taken from nearby ironworks.

The iron was produced in domed 'bloomery' furnaces made from clay strengthened with stone, within which the temperature would be raised to 1,000°C, using several pairs of manually operated bellows blowing on a fire and charcoal base, often for days on end. Once the desired temperature had been reached, small chunks of ore, mined from pits, and an equal amount of charcoal were added. This was repeated over a lengthy period of time until metallic iron began to collect in the base, having partly separated from the waste slag.

The spongy masses of iron (blooms) were then extracted and over a heated forge, hammered vigorously until the last of the entrapped slag had been expelled, leaving iron that could then be turned into tools, weapons, nails, chains, buckles and other domestic ironwork.

The Romans brought with them a variation on furnace design where a shaft was set into a bank of clay or sand. Those Roman workings in the west, and at that time Broadfields (Crawley) appears to be the most westerly, seemed to cater for the domestic market, and were run by civilians. Those in the east, including Barndown (Ticehurst), Footlands (Sedlescombe) and Chitcombe

(Brede), appear to have been large scale thriving businesses with lucrative markets in London to where products were probably moved by water, possibly via the Brede estuary or the Rother. There is much to suggest that the workings were so well funded and well organised that they may have been supported by the state or came under the authority of 'Classis Britannica', the Roman fleet.

But by the first half of the third century, the Wealden iron industry, one of Britain's principal exports, started to decline. A number of large workings, such as at Beauport Park (Battle/Westfield), which had been supplying quantities of iron through Dover for Roman legions in Europe, were forced to close because of constant forays by Channel pirates, coupled with the silting-up of the river estuaries. The Forest of Dean in Gloucestershire, another prime iron producing area, was looked upon more favourably, being in a safer location and producing economically-priced iron.

By the end of the third century, only sites at Oldlands (Maresfield), Broadfields(Crawley) and Footlands (Sedlescombe) appear to have survived, although they, too, soon fell into disuse.

After the Romans had been hustled out of England in 410AD by the Anglo-Saxons, there seems to have been little interest in re-establishing iron workings in Sussex. A mere handful of bloomeries continued, confirmed by one, Millbrook, on Ashdown Forest, which was excavated and radiocarbon-dated to the ninth century. And the Domesday Survey of 1086 mentions only one iron works (ferraria), at East Grinstead.

The extraction of ore and the production of iron in the county was not revived until the middle of the 13th century. Workings in the Forest of Dean had the monopoly of iron production for some two centuries, but by 1250 the Crown had started to purchase iron objects from Wealden forges and furnaces. Nails, and bars, spikes for wheels, horseshoes and arrows and arrowheads. Horsham was an area specialising in arrows. In 1253 Henry III turned to the Sheriff of Sussex seeking 30,000 horseshoes and 60,000 nails for the royal army, and in 1266 he granted the town of Lewes the right to levy a toll on 'every cart laden with iron from the neighbouring weald, for sale, paid one penny toll and on every horse-load of iron half that sum'. But local supplies were so short that requirements for iron at Lewes in 1270 had to be met by the importation of Spanish iron through the port of Winchelsea. Bar iron was also sold to estate smiths to be worked and used for repairing carts and ploughs.

With regional economy expanding, local needs for iron products grew. But this period of activity was suddenly curtailed by the Black Death, the great bubonic plague of 1349. This time of great mortality brought with it much

A Wealden gun forge, showing charcoal loading at the top left; chipping clean a complete casting, below; and lowering a mould into a gun pit, centre. On the right is the water wheel that powers the forge machinery.
From a drawing by RJ Adams

disruption. Food became expensive, workforces were dimished. Many labourers were able to pick and choose better paid jobs. To be able to fulfil their orders furnace owners had to offer generous wages, sometimes as much as fifty per cent above pre-Black Death rates.

But the industry recovered and appeared to flourish as in 1379 tax returns for the Crawley area show a William Rokenham, a 'factor ferri' assessed at the high rate of 6s 8d and a William Danecombe 40s.

By the 1490s numbers of immigrant French workers were arriving bringing with them their skills in iron technology. Both the Crown and the expanding markets of London and the south east were demanding iron armaments and wrought iron goods.

The most significant advance in the history of Wealden iron was in December 1496 with the introduction from the Low Countries of the first water powered blast furnace and forge at Newbridge ironworks, built on Duchy of Lancaster land on Ashdown Forest. There had been a bloomery on the site previously, taking full advantage of the natural resources – plenty of wood, water and ore. Utilising water power and the skills of immigrant ironworkers, the new furnace and forge could turn out at least ten times as much iron as its predecessor. Within a year the workings were up and running, completing orders for iron and shot for the King's artillery in its Scottish campaign.

Equally there was a growing demand for iron products for buildings, especially in London. South east England's agriculture also enjoyed prosperity as the capital needed food supplies. Thus farmers were able to spend money on new equipment or new buildings. By 1548 some thirty-two furnaces and thirty-eight forges had sprung up in the Weald to cope with the demand for iron products and armaments.

The Wealden iron industry had now entered one of its most prosperous eras and Sussex was, until almost the time of Queen Victoria, the most industrialised county in England. Except for agriculture, the iron industry was the oldest and most continuous in the Weald. (See Appendix 4).

Under the reign of Henry VIII the production of iron became more than just a small local industry. Wealden iron bars appear to have been sold around the country. The county grew rich on the outpourings of the furnaces. The owners and ironmasters grew wealthy. Many families rose up the social scale, names well known in the iron industry – Fowle, Fuller, Carryll, Pelham and Neville. In 1549 the iron mills of Sheffield (Fletching) employed twenty-three labourers; at Worth, where there was a double furnace for gun founding, thirty-three workers are recorded, and forty-nine are mentioned at Edward Caryll's St Leonards (Lower Beeding) furnace and forge. By 1664 there was a generous, but perhaps over enthusiastic, estimation that some 50,000 men were employed in the county.

The historian Camden wrote of the reign of Queen Elizabeth: 'It is full of iron mines, for the casting of which there are furnaces up and down the country, and abundance of wood is yearly spent: many streams are drawn into one channel, and a great deal of meadow ground is turned into ponds for the driving of mills by the flashes which, beating with hammers upon the iron, fill the neighbourhood round about, night and day, with continued noise. But the iron wrought here is not everywhere of the same goodness, yet generally more brittle than the Spanish, whether it be from nature, or tincture and temper; nevertheless, the proprietors of the mines, by casting of cannon and other things, make them turn to good account. But whether the nation is in anyway advantaged by them, is a doubt which the next age will be able to resolve.'

Much of the income from the furnaces was derived from the export of arms. So much high class ordnance was finding its way into the hands of possible enemies, especially Spain, that steps were taken, albeit in the main, unsuccessfully, to stop their export. Frequently shipments of contraband were seized; in one case a John Harman of Lewes was caught exporting twenty-six 'sacars and miniones' worth £312. Undeterred, the smugglers carried on, doing a roaring trade chasing handsome profits.

Not only were Wealden iron products in demand abroad, skilled furnace workers were approached with tempting offers to work for foreign employers.

Whilst the iron industry thrived and prospered, it was at the expense of Wealden timber, which was being felled at an alarming rate to produce furnace charcoal. The ports of Rye, Winchelsea and Hastings complained that the profits from their timber exporting trade had dropped dramatically because the wood was being burnt on Wealden furnaces. And in 1577, when similar complaints were voiced about a foundry at Westfield, Lord Buckhurst retaliated by saying they had no right to complain as during the last two years they had exported 'not so little as 1,000 tons of timber'.

Initially there seemed little interest in replacing the trees that had been used. Regenerative coppicing only came later when landowners began to realise that there was much to be recommended for maintaining rather than demolishing their woodlands. Deciduous trees began to be appreciated as a renewable resource, bringing in a continuous source of income. Branches with eight to twelve years' growth could be cut and several new shoots would appear from the stump. So the management of woodlands grew as the iron industry developed. About 4,000 acres of coppiced woodland were required for each ironworks. Any astute businessman entering the iron manufacturing market had to be certain of guaranteed supplies of wood. Furnaces and woodlands were often leased together as a packaged deal. No timber, no business.

Besides the iron industry needing wood, the glass makers and shipbuilders were in direct competition for diminishing supplies, so in 1558, 1581 and 1585, Parliamentary Acts were passed regulating the cutting of wood for use in furnaces. This in turn, pushed up the price of charcoal, but the ironmasters seemed well able to meet the rising prices. A cynical comment from the Admiralty about this situation suggested that 'as so much wood was being used up in the production of naval guns there was a real danger that there might be no further ships built to put them on'.

Between 1548 and 1573 the number of Wealden ironworks had doubled from fifty-three to 110, seven of which were casting ordnance. The industry, now well capable of supplying bar and cast iron to an ever growing market, had extended geographically north eastwards into Wealden Kent, to Lamberhurst, Horsmonden, Hawkhurst and Tonbridge.

Bars of iron were supplied either to local smiths or sold in bulk, often to large London ironmongery businesses, the iron from south east areas often shipped out from Rye and Newhaven, also Pevensey, where warehouses had been specially built.

From the central Weald, the routes to London undertaken by the ironmasters' heavy wagons were along unmade, narrow highways, which were 'hard as iron in summer, thick as soup in winter'.

An Act of 1585 'for the Amendment of High Waies decaied by carriage to and fro Yron Mylles' stipulated that persons carrying charcoal, ore or iron between October 12 and May 1 should carry for every six loads of 'coales or mine' and for every ton of iron 'one usuale carte loade of sinder, gravell, stone, sande, or chalke, meate for the repairing and the amendinge of the said Highways'. A further Act of 1597 required everyone carrying charcoal, ore or iron, to pay to a justice of the peace a highway rate of for every three loads or ton of iron. Further, anyone carrying thirty loads or ten tons of iron would have to lay, between May 1 and October 12, one load of cinder, gravel, chalk or stone. There was a ten shilling penalty if the Act were ignored.

The Civil War, between King Charles I and Parliament, which started in 1642, brought fresh problems to the ironmasters. To which side should they pledge their iron and guns? Although much of the Wealden area was in the hands of the Parliamentarians, there was little military activity in Sussex. But suppliers to the Office or Ordnance, such as John Browne, the king's gunstonemaker, were naturally committed to supplying the Royalist side with arms. It has though, been suggested that John Browne hedged his bets and may well have supplied both sides during certain periods of the war. A few ironworks whose owners were known to have Royalist affinities were put out of action.

After the Civil war there appears to have been a shift in the relationships between furnaces and forges. The furnaces could turn out bar iron (pig iron) and sell it on to be converted elsewhere. But with various wars rumbling around not a few ironmasters took the view that it might be prudent, and profitable, to start casting ordnance, especially since quality, competitively priced foreign iron, particularly from the Baltic and later Sweden and Spain, was also being imported in increasing quantities. Not only that, forges in the Midlands had begun to enter the picture, and smiths there were selling their tools, locks, chains and nails cheaper, undercutting those in the south east.

The pig iron was, in many cases, set aside in favour of guns and shot. A number of London investors could see the potential of leasing Wealden furnaces, as could a consortium of ironmasters from the Midlands, 'Ironworks in Partnership'. Prosperity was written on the wall.

There were plenty of takers for Office of Ordnance contracts although the Office's quality requirements were steep, their orders erratic and their payments slow. But for some furnaces, money coming in from supplying ordnance to the military provided a generous dollop of jam on the bread and butter of everyday iron items. Sub-contracting, co-operatives and split orders eased the cash flow problems.

In 1710 Richard Jones of Lamberhurst Furnace obtained an order for 200 tons of iron railings cast for St Paul's Cathedral, at a cost, with fixing, of £11,430 12s 9d. Part of this order he sub-contracted to other Wealden ironworks, and he delivered the railings by water. The railings were described in *Hasted's Kent* (1782): 'They compose the most magnificent balustrade perhaps in the universe, being of the height of five feet six inches, at which there are at intervals seven iron gates of beautiful workmanship, which altogether weigh 200 tons 81lbs.'

The merchant trade was an equally profitable outlet, although some questionable ethics were involved when a batch of guns rejected by the Office of Ordnance, which should have been destroyed, found their way into arms destined for the merchant fleets.

And, of course, there was the export trade. Requirements here were mostly for guns. In 1736 the King of Portugal was a customer; in 1752 the Queen of Hungary ordered 100 tons, as did the King of Sardinia, who offered cash on delivery. Although the greater majority of furnaces did not at that time appear to be producing ordnance, most were casting ammunition, often in quantity.

During the last years of the Seven Years War, which ended in 1763, the Wealden iron industry went through its final period of major activity. Ordnance was still in demand, much of it for the merchant trade, although there was some dangerous competition for the regular markets from founders in the Midlands and Wales. The Carron Company from Scotland, hoping for a generous share of the arms market, began cutting prices of their guns by £5 a ton, which they

Sections of the railings at St Paul's Cathedral, London, were removed in 1874 after many people were crushed against them at the Thanksgiving for the recovery of the Prince of Wales from illness. The small section illustrated is in the Gun Garden at Lewes Castle

could afford to do as their furnaces were now powered by the more economical coke. Confronted with diminishing supplies of wood, increased competition from outside and an inability of the owners to think progressively, the bottom finally fell out of Wealden iron industry with the closing of the last forge at Ashburnham in 1813.

The Sussex iron industry was revived in a comparatively small way when John Every opened an iron foundry at Lewes in 1831. Shortly afterwards it burnt down but Every started again with the aptly named Phoenix Iron Works. This started in a small building at the foot of North Street. The equipment was basic, the furnace blast supplied by a horse walking round and round to keep a fan in motion. At the time there were two other iron works in Lewes, Morris and Thompson, but while Phoenix grew and prospered the rivals declined and eventually went out of business.

By 1935 the fourth and fifth generation Everys were running extensive workshops, a smithy, assembly bays, foundry and an iron museum (now at Anne of Cleves House Museum in Lewes). In the early 1950s the ironworks passed into the hands of East Sussex Engineering Company.

A fireplace with all the accessories at the Phoenix Ironworks museum

15

GUN-MAKING

Out of the Weald, the secret Weald,
Men sent in ancient years,
The horse-shoes red at Flodden Field,
The arrows of Potiers.
See you the dimpled track that runs
All hollow through the wheat?
O that was where they hauled the guns
that smote King Philip's fleet.

When Philip II's Spanish Armada sailed up the English Channel in July 1588, to be met by Sir Francis Drake and Howard of Effingham, contrary to popular opinion not only were Wealden-made cast iron guns evident on the 120 auxiliary ships of the English fleet, they also formed a good part of the armament of the opposing Spanish fleet.

For some 300 years Sussex cast iron guns were considered to be the finest in the world. Historian David Hyme, in *History of England*, wrote: 'Ship building and the founding of iron cannon were the sole arts in which England excelled'. But the industry was restricted by political intrigue, prejudice, erratic sales and conservation lobbyists determined to stop the mass destruction of trees for furnace charcoal.

Guns were first used in warfare in the early 1300s and although they were being actively manufactured on the Continent, England was slow to follow. The first blast furnace and forge capable of turning them out appeared in Sussex in 1496, built on Crown property at Newbridge in the parish of Hartfield.

Henry VII needed military supplies to equip his army for the invasion of Scotland, and the Weald, with its advantageous location, suitable iron ore, specialist workforce and vast forests was in a favourable position to accommodate him.

In 1498, Frenchman, Pauncelett Symart, a skilled gun-maker took out a seven year lease, at £20 a year, on the Newbridge furnace. One of many French immigrants ironworkers, he attempted to make iron guns, although the design of brittle wrought iron strips bound together by metal hoops, often proved more lethal to their users than to the enemy, having a tendency to explode when used. A year later he must have been reasonably successful in his attempts to make a two-part gun as he sent guns to Portsmouth to arm one of Henry's new navy ships, *Le Sovereign*.

The unreliability of the first iron guns, coupled with their corrosive qualities, meant that sales of bronze guns being produced on the Continent were far greater. Although they were relatively easy to cast, were strong and light, they quickly wore out and, as was to prove so advantageous to later Wealden gunfounders, extremely expensive, being up to four times as costly as iron guns.

Although the Tower of London placed an order in 1508 for 'Gonnes of iron late caste in the fforest of Ashdowne in the Countic of Sussex' orders were slow and by 1509 the Newbridge works had been run down. Symart moved out in 1512 and Humphrey Walker, the King's founder, moved in. He appears to have produced only bullets for the monarch's bronze guns.

At Parrock in the parish of Hartfield, Robert and Richard Scorer were turning out iron munitions, and in 1510 Richard was given the appointment of King's Gunstonemaker.

When Henry VIII came to the throne in 1509 he appears to have had little interest in buying Wealden guns, preferring to spend money from the royal coffers on proven bronze ordnance from the Continent. Within two decades he had bought 140 bronze guns from the Flemish gunfounder Poppenruyter, in Malines, including the well known bombards called the Twelve Apostles.

A Tudor demi-culver, late 16th century, carrying the royal cypher of Elizabeth I on the barrel. This weapon, which may be seen at Pevensey Castle, could fire a 9lb shot a distance of up to 400 yards

He acquired or built twenty-four ships and armed them with bronze guns. With all this military and naval re-equipment Henry overstretched himself financially and, by 1522, he had to look around for more economic alternatives. In a change of policy he decided that bronze guns could be made more cheaply in England and he engaged the services of experienced foreign gunfounders to work foundries in and around London. One of these was Peter Baude, an outstanding French craftsman who was employed at the Bell House foundry in Houndsditch, working with brothers John and Robert Owen. They, along with the Italian Arcano family from Salisbury Place foundry, London, were responsible for the superb bronze cannon with which the ill-fated *Mary Rose*, Henry VIII's greatest warship, was equipped. The ship sank near Portsmouth on her maiden voyage on July 19, 1545.

Henry, a man of imperious will, proclaimed himself Supreme Head of the English Church, an action which brought an aggressive response from Pope Pius III, threatening excommunication. In 1538 the pontiff attempted an alliance between Spain and France to form a crusade against the King.

In the face of this threatened invasion Henry set about building a string of forts and blockhouses from Tilbury to Cornwall at a cost of £375,000. By 1540 he had completed some twenty-nine castles and bulwarks along the most vulnerable points of the south east coast and eighteen had been provided with gunners.

Although the invasion never came, by 1542 the country was again at war with Scotland and by 1543 with France. Henry urgently needed large supplies of armament at an economic cost. There was much to recommend sustained efforts by the Wealden iron foundries to find a successful method of producing reliable iron guns cast in one piece as the bronze guns were.

There were only ever a handful of men actively involved in the production of guns, turning them out from a small number of Sussex furnaces. The 'father' of these was Parson William Levett. An ambitious cleric, he was Rector of Guestling and West Dean before moving to Buxted in 1533, where he was appointed Deputy to the Receiver of the King's Revenue in Sussex.

Shortly afterwards, his elder brother John died, leaving in his will a number of iron mills and furnaces to his son, also John. Under the terms of the will, executed by William Levett, the furnaces were to be rented out until John junior came of age and in 1543 a John Levett became the lessee of a furnace at Stumlet or Stumblett, west of Newbridge. Although there is no documentary evidence to support this, it is believed that William Levett, in between his ecclesiastical duties, may have managed this for a number of years, obtaining a great deal of experience with blast furnaces.

The second person to enter into experimental gunfounding was Ralph

Hogge, an employee of Levetts. Born in the village of Maresfield, he was ambitious, and, in spite of the fact he could neither read nor write, he went on to become an experienced gunfounder and probably attained the position of furnace master.

On May 13, 1560, Hogge married Margaret Henslowe at St Bartholomew's Church, Maresfield. This appears to have been an arranged marriage, as Hogge was some twenty years older than his bride and of a lower class. He may have seen the marriage as a convenient way up the social ladder with opportunities of finding ready financial investment in his iron works. The Henslowes, being gentry, astutely saw the prospects of financial benefit from what promised to be a lucrative business.

A display at Anne of Cleves House, Lewes, showing the boring of a gun

The third character was the French craftsman from Houndsditch, Peter Baude who had become a successful maker of bronze ordnance, regularly supplying the Crown.

Encouraged by the government, Baude, Levett and Hogge pooled their respective talents of gunmaker, furnace owner and experienced founder to find a way of successfully casting a safe one piece iron gun at the Buxted works. In 1543, a significant date in gun making history, after many attempts and numerous testings on Hawkhurst's Gun Green, the trio perfected the technique of casting one-piece iron guns that would rival bronze. This gave rise to the couplet:

Master Huggett and his man John
They did cast the first cannon

Although no records exist of the process they used it is widely recognised that the use of loam instead of sand in the moulds meant it was possible to apply a greater heat for drying. A good, dry mould stopped steam evaporating when liquid iron came into contact with the loam, thus eliminating bubbles of air from the metal.

Guns were urgently needed for the coastal artillery forts and there was a great call for firearms. But Henry and the experts of naval ordnance were were still wary of the new iron guns, perhaps suspicious of their long standing problems, although by 1545, with the imminent threat of a French invasion, Levett was urged to deliver as much shot and as many guns as he could.

At this point Archbishop Cranmer evicted Levett from his Buxted parsonage and deprived him of his appointment as Rector. Just after Christmas in 1546 Levett was commissioned to oversee Sussex ironworks belonging to the Duke of Norfolk. One was at Sheffield in the parish of Fletching, the second, and more important, was near the village of Worth at Crawley. Here Levett constructed a double furnace which was capable of turning out sufficient molten iron at one time to cast much larger guns.

In a ten year period from 1540 to 1550 there was a rapid expansion to twenty-one active furnaces in the Weald. Levett was casting guns at Buxted and Worth, a Robert Hodson at Poundsey furnace, Framfield and an Arthur Middleton at Huggetts in Buxted Parish. The others were all supplying iron implements to farming communities and iron goods to London.

For the gunfounders, after the high, came the low. By 1550 the country was at peace with both Scotland and France. Henry had died in 1547, Queen Mary now reigned. And, ominously, two new rival blast furnaces had opened up in Kent and Surrey.

The ironworks were also facing attack from the ports of Hastings, Rye and Winchelsea, which, in 1548, complained that their extremely profitable timber exporting trade was drying up by being burnt up in the expanding number of some fifty ironworks.

Michael Drayton, a local conservationist of his day, wrote:

> *'Jove's oak, the war-like ash,veined elm, the softer beech,*
> *Short hazel, maple plain, light asp and bending wych,*
> *What should the builder serve, supplies the forger's turn,*
> *When under public good, base private gain takes hold,*
> *And we, poor woeful woods, to ruin lastly sold.'*

Wealden gunfounders were also unpopular with naval shipbuilders and the glass making industry, both of whom were in competition for depleting timber supplies. And at this time the gunfounders were just about surviving by supplying guns to the merchant fleet which needed economic defensive ordnance to protect their trade routes.

In 1554 William Levett died, leaving Ralph Hogge 'the sum of four pounds and six tonne of sows (long pieces of cast iron)' in his will. As Levett's principal furnace master and founder, Hogge naturally stepped into his master's shoes. By 1559 he had become widely recognised as a skilled maker of guns and shot and was given the grant for life of 'maker of ironstone for guns', to be supplied to the Office of Ordnance in the Tower of London, a position that paid a fee of sixpence a day.

After Mary's death in 1558, Elizabeth I came to the throne. Between 1559 and 1564 she began an active policy of building or buying fifteen new naval vessels, but like her father, Henry VIII, she made little attempt to arm them with Wealden cast iron guns, probably influenced by the continuing preferences for bronze by the purchasers of naval ordnance.

But if Queen and country were not overly interested in buying the Wealden guns, there were others prepared to pay good money for them and no questions asked. Spanish and French pirates became increasingly interested in these cheaper cast iron guns which could easily be purchased through ports on the south east coast. Dutch Calvanists were fighting the Spanish as privateers. They too, needed arms. A flourishing and lucrative trade in Sussex guns began flowing to the Continent, perhaps as much as three quarters of the output of Wealden furnaces. This situation began to worry the government, which foresaw serious military danger and damage to national security. The Low Countries, France, Spain and Portugal were all trying to lay their hands on English cast iron guns. There was a resurgence in the industry, the number of gun furnaces increased from four to eight or nine, and more new furnaces appeared outside the Weald, namely in Glamorgan, Monmouth, Shropshire and Staffordshire.

Ralph Hogge was given exclusive rights in 1568 to manufacturer guns and shot for export. In theory this was to be done under the watchful eye of the Master of Ordnance. But other gunfounders, eager for a share of this now extremely lucrative trade, soon found ways around this ban. Thus, by 1573, Wealden iron production was reaching an all time high, forcing Hogge to complain to the Privy Council that because of unauthorised export of guns abroad 'hostile vessels were becoming better armed than English ships'.

He pointed out how easily guns could be turned out from furnaces claiming to be making iron bars, and smuggled across the Channel in clandestine shipments often, straight into enemy hands. There were also agents willing to handle Wealden ordnance of any shape or size, confident they could eventually sell it to any interested party at a good profit.

This produced a thorough survey by the Privy Council of the ironworks of the Weald and from this, in 1574, in a move to protect the realm, it issued a blanket veto stopping the sale of all guns abroad. This was later replaced with a control system that, being underfunded, was largely ineffective.The gunfounders, agents and middlemen soon found ways around the embargo, mostly the time honoured Sussex trade of smuggling. Wealden guns were still being daily shipped abroad, often aided by corrupt officials.

Most of Spain's fighting ships carried bronze guns, but she badly needed more ordnance. Wealden cast iron guns were the only source of supply. Spanish agents in Flanders were offering £19-22 a ton for iron guns against the market price of £10-12. Small wonder that many English merchants were prepared to smuggle guns out. In 1591 there was fourteen cases of contraband seizure at Lewes and Newhaven.

Even after the defeat of the Spanish Armada, Spain was still actively seeking supplies with which to arm a new fleet for another invasion. The Privy Council desperately tried to halt the flow. In 1592 the Master of Ordnance was given wide powers to oversee and control the forges and furnaces. But by the end of the century clandestine shipments were again carrying guns abroad, frequently to Spain. Foreign vessels often smuggled guns out as ballast. Again, government restrictions seemed to be little more than another paper exercise. In spite of the risks, good money and high profits in a bouyant market proved much too attractive.

From the early 1600s there was a substantial shift towards the use of iron guns on warships. Much of this ordnance was supplied by founder John Browne, whose father, Thomas Browne, had owned furnaces at Bough Beech, Chiddingstone, Ashurst and

Horam's village sign, made of wood and wrought iron, and showing a man fashioning a cannon, was made to celebrate the jubilee of George V and Queen Mary, hence the GM beneath the crown

Horsmonden, and who had been a gunfounder to the Crown, with large scale business commitments with the military and mercantile.

Merchant shipping involved in long distance trading needed ordnance to tackle the growing problems of piracy. The East India Company, in particular, armed most of its fleet with guns purchased from Thomas Browne.

His son John succeeded to the title of the King's Gunstonemaker in 1615. An astute businessman, he endeavoured to keep the gun making business ticking over efficiently, a difficult task with irregular requirements from the Crown and irregular payments for goods delivered. Cash flow was a problem even then. More than once John Browne refused to hand over completed orders until previous accounts had been settled. He often had to turn to making other iron products, such as firebacks and graveslabs, in times of peace to keep his skilled workforce in employment.

He experimented with iron guns and in the mid-1620s eventually managed to produce some that were lighter than bronze using a 'refined metal'. They proved popular and were sold in large quantities to merchants. He then started to cast bronze guns at the Horsmunden furnace using recycled old guns.

Although the Brownes kept the Crown supplied with ordnance they still needed additional income from the export trade. In 1613 Elias Trippe approached Thomas Browne with an order for 200 iron guns for the Netherlands. With Privy Council permission and correct document-ation this business arrangement cont-inued until 1618 when the govern-ment, fearing too many guns were being channelled to doubtful destin-ations and the stock level of arms in England was getting dangerously low, decided to

Above is one of two replica guns on display in the Gun Garden at the Ypres Tower Museum, Rye. They were cast by Rye Foundry and built by Ian Wood of Playden. In July 1980 the guns were presented to Queen Elizabeth the Queen Mother, Warden of the Cinque Ports, on her eightieth birthday.

terminate the permission to export. Skilled workers, too, were being induced to give their services to foreign employers.

This gave the emerging Swedish ordnance industry, with their government's encouragement, the opportunity to step in and sell low priced arms in Europe. In retaliation, John Browne tried, albeit unsuccessfully, with the support of the Lords of the Admiralty, to petition the King to prohibit the import of all Swedish cast iron items into England.

The Civil War meant that Wealden gunfounders had to decide which side their loyalty and their guns lay. John Browne, as a supplier to the Office of Ordnance, appears to have chosen, in the main, to equip the Royalist side. His employees were not pressed into military service so orders could be fulfilled. In 1641 he was given the use of the Royal ironworks in the Forest of Dean.

There had been a gradual spread of blast furnaces into South Wales and the West Midlands, London merchants were buying the cheaper, although inferior, Swedish iron. The numbers of Wealden furnaces began to decrease, the survivors being gunfounders kept in business by continuing conflicts.

Some formed a type of co-operative. With the outbreak of war in 1739 a long-standing iron founder, William Harrison, joined up with William and George Jukes at Robertsbridge furnace and in 1741 formed a partnership with a Wadhurst founder, John Legas.

A neighbour of William Harrison was London merchant Samuel Remnant who worked a foundry at Woolwich, adjacent to the Royal Arsenal. Here he manufactured iron goods and also round shot, for which the Board of Ordnance was an excellent customer. Not one to miss an opportunity Remnant offered to act as an agent for Harrison and the Fuller family, of Heathfield furnace, negotiating deals on their behalf with the Board and subcontracting advantageously in order to complete lucrative contracts. This integration of several gunfounders seemed to work well until the late 1740s when John Fuller became suspicious that Remnant was 'apparently not working in their best interests' and moved to another agent. Not long afterwards Samuel Remant was accused, along with a number of Board of Ordnance officials, of defrauding the Board out of some £10,000.

The fortunes of Wealden gunfounders took an upturn with the start of the Seven Years War in 1756, although this proved to be the last period of major activity for the industry. In anticipation of hostilities and therefore desperate for large quantities of guns and shot, the Board of Ordnance contacted the gunfounders early in the year asking what arms they could supply and how quickly. Fuller, amongst others, saw the opportunity to negotiate higher prices. The Board was in no position to argue and agreed, although it imposed stricter conditions on deliveries, threatening not to pay at all for uncompleted orders.

Fuller, Harrison and his new partner, John Churchill, urged the Board to make six-monthly payments because with so much money tied up in stock, they could be subject to cash flow problems.

The higher payments for ordnance soon caught the attention of ironmasters outside the Weald. Businesses in Sowley (Hampshire), Carmarthen, Neath and Bristol all sought a piece of the action. But most were small time with little long term experience. Often quality was too poor to pass the Board's rigorous proofing tests or orders were delivered late. Most withdrew. One that was successful was John Wilkinson, from North Wales. His entry into the gunfounding business was to have great significance later.

Naturally, more furnaces opened up in the Weald. One of note was at Gravetye, West Hoathly, owned by William Clutton and John Norden. They sub-contracted to make guns and shot for the London merchants Eade and Wilton, King Edward Stairs, Wapping. Jonathan Eade and William Wilton had supplied the Board of Ordnance with guns and shot since the beginning of the previous war. They do not appear to have made ordnance themselves, but acted as agents for gunfounders, including Wilkinson from Wales and the Fuller family of Heathfield.

Three years into the war the Board had managed to purchase enough guns so, by 1760, few further orders were received by the gun founders. And although the demand rose slightly when Spain entered the conflict in 1762, when peace was declared in 1763 orders from the Board virtually ceased and prices slumped.

Most founders had been prepared for this and found alternative outlets with domestic requirements and the merchant trade, restrictions having been lifted. At this point Roebuck and Company, from the Carron ironworks at Falkirk, made a calculated gamble to seize business. In November 1754 it offered to cast guns and shot for the Board for the low price of £14 a ton. This was accepted. Other gun founders were not prepared to do so, still riding high on the great profits made during wartime.

Badly hit were the Fullers from Heathfield and William Clutton from Gravetye, who had no other outlets and relied solely on contracts with the Board, both in war and peace. Inevitably some gunfounders were forced out of business, others like Clutton and Tapsell, went bankrupt.

The demise of Richard Tapsell had far reaching effects. He had been brought into the Harrison business after Harrison's death in 1745. As a nephew of the wife of John Legas, one of the trustees of the estate, he was appointed to take his place and help run the estate alongside John and Andrew Harrison, William's sons. The partnership had embraced five furnaces and when Tapsall went bankrupt at least fifty per cent of the active Wealden ironworks were, for a time, closed.

Outside the Weald both Wilkinson and the Carron Company had begun to use the more economic coke for smelting. They had built their businesses up with a view to running them bigger and better and long term, whereas Wealden furnaces had thrived and prospered in the short term but with little investment in their future. The Carron Company, between 1765 and 1770 supplied the Board of Ordnance with guns worth £22,000. Some Wealden gunfounders, like the powerful Fullers, had failed to diversify in times of peace. Much of the iron making industry began to migrate to the Midlands and the North in the face of depleted supplies of wood and intense cut price competition from outside by users of the more cost effective coal or coke.

The final blow came when the Board of Ordnance, in 1773, insisted on the boring of solid cast guns. A decade later gunfounding in the Weald ceased altogether.

16

IRON GRAVESLABS

A minor sideline of the Wealden iron industry during the sixteenth, seventeenth and early eighteenth centuries was the manufacture of graveslabs – thin slabs, or 'ledgers' of metal some 6ftx2ftx2in, which were used to cover graves, usually those inside churches.

Although they are a peculiarity of the Weald they are not unique to the area. Others have been found near ironworks in Wales and the West Midlands. But by far the greatest number of the 100 that now remain are to be found in some twenty Sussex churches. The parish church of St Peter and St Paul at Wadhurst, in the heart of iron country, can boast thirty-three slabs.

Most slabs are in churches close to ironworks. They were made individually to memorialise the more affluent ironmasters and their relatives. The earliest known graveslab is c1537 at Burwash; it is long and narrow with a small cross in relief.

Like firebacks, graveslabs were made by the simple process of creating a mould of sand and impressing letters or pattern blocks into the sand bed. Molten iron was then poured in and the impressions would then give a relief image on the graveslab.

In theory this appeared a simple process, but the foundry workers or apprentices were unschooled and often illiterate. Many graveslabs bear evidence of their mistakes. Where movable letter moulds were used, letters such as 'S' or 'F' were reversed and uneducated casters, unable to read, or understand words correctly, often just impressed lines of letters regardless of meaning. Their job was made doubly difficult because the die-blocks had to have the details carved on them in reverse so the finished graveslab read correctly.

Richard Infield's graveslab at West Hoathly is unique in that the inscription runs around the border.

Apart from letter moulds, blocks were made containing heraldic devices, coats of arms and crests. These were often used more than once. The same family crest for the Fowles (Riverhall furnace, Wadhurst) appears on graveslabs at both Frant and Wadhurst. The Frant slab is dated 1631 and a fireback in the Hastings Museum has the same crest dated 1603.

By the eighteenth century incised lettering, cut with a chisel, had become more common. The words could be added at any time without the disadvantages of working out the details before casting and being applied in reverse.

The iron grave slab of David Barham – who died on February 18, 1643 – on the parish church at Wadhurst. The slab also records the death in 1688 of another Barham, identified only as AB

As firebacks and graveslabs were markedly similar they were sometimes erroneously interchanged. And with the passage of time some have moved far away from their original use. In East Grinstead a graveslab cast for Anne Barclay (1570) had been used as a scullery step and at Anne of Cleves Museum there is a graveslab to Robert Baker (1585) that came from a Sevenoaks bakery where it had been used as an ashplate for the bakery furnace. Robert Baker had owned Hamsell Furnace, Rotherfield in 1583.

By the eighteenth century, with the movement of the iron industry northwards, Wealden graveslabs were being replaced by marble and the few that are now to be seen in churches or museums are the last vestiges of a once great Sussex industry.

17

IRON FIREBACKS

A by-product of the Wealden iron industry were firebacks, slabs of decorated iron to set at the back of fireplaces and inglenooks.

Before the end of the fifteenth century timber-framed houses had open fires for heating and cooking in the centre of their living rooms. There were no chimneys, the smoke had to find its way out through doors and windows.

By the end of the fifteenth century the fires had moved back against the walls with chimneys above and large brick or stone fireplaces built around them to lessen the chances of accidental fires. But the fires often attacked the soft brickwork. Large square or rectangular slabs of Wealden iron laid up against the back wall provided the perfect and lasting solution as well as being a superb reservoir of heat.

The firebacks were simple to cast. Wooden boards cut to the required size were pressed down into a bed of loam or sand to form a mould. Molten iron was then run in and allowed to cool.

Most firebacks can be dated by their embellishments and, to some extent, their size. Some of the first were wider than they were high and were decorated with simple designs. Pieces of twisted rope, stiffened with pitch, were impressed into the mould which gave a pattern in relief. This twisted cable was a common characteristic of the 15th and 16th century firebacks and many had rope decoration edging round the top and two sides, although not at the bottom; this was not considered necessary as that part of the fireback would be covered by the fire.

Later, more ambitious designs came about with the use of small wooden blocks carved with popular fleur-de-lys or coats of arms which could be pressed into the loam or sand a number of times, at the whim of the moulders attempting to produce some kind of repeating pattern. The results, although interesting, were often crooked or upside-down.

As the big fires and big fireplaces gradually became smaller, so did firebacks. They became, in the main, square. There was now a huge range of subjects that were being used for decoration. Large single, detailed pattern moulds, perhaps created by more experienced hands, were repeatedly used to cope with an expanding market.

A notable fireback that is full of detail can be seen at Anne of Cleves House Museum in Lewes. It was cast at the Brede furnace by iron founder Richard

Lenard, and it shows him surrounded by the many tools of his trade and a dog jumping up at him. His initials, RL, are set within a model fireback in the bottom right hand corner. Over his head are the words:

RICHARD LENARD AT BRED FOURNIS 1636

The equipment he used, shown on the fireback, are a heavy hammer to break up the iron ore before placing into the furnace; a wheelbarrow; a woodstack for fuel; a charcoal basket; a cauldron and cast-iron weight; a ladle; flaggons and tankards; a small hammer; a firedog; a cast iron weight; pinchers; a blast furnace; a Tuyere hook for removing lumps or iron.

Another somewhat gruesome fireback on display in Lewes depicts the death of Richard Woodman and the Sussex Martyrs at Lewes. Richard Woodman was an wealthy but deeply religious ironmaster from Warbleton who, in 1554, was imprisoned for his almost fanatical Protestant beliefs. Once released he refused to be silenced and finding out there was a warrant for his arrest he fled into the Sussex countryside and eventually travelled to Flanders. His brother looked after the ironworks but appears to have embezzled some £200. To try and clear up the problems of the missing money Richard Woodman returned home only to be discovered hiding under the roof of his house. Ironically, in his haste to escape, he cut his feet on sharp cinders from his own furnace. He was tried and, along with others who refused to alter their beliefs, burned at the stake.

A third fireback, of which only a half is at Anne of Cleves House,

The Richard Leonard fireback at Anne of Cleves House Museum

The Lewes Martyrs fireback

depicts the defeat of the Spanish Armada in 1588. It would appear that a number of these were produced as a complete specimen was held at Lewes's Phoenix Ironworks Museum, and another was discovered in the early 1950s set in a large fireplace that had been covered by a smaller fireplace at Woods Mill, Small Dole.

The use of coal for fires instead of wood had become well established in the Wealden area by the middle of the 18th century. Its introduction, along with fire grates, radically altered the shape of firebacks which eventually became mere tall, thin iron plates, although their decoration was often even more detailed, many showing classical figures.

Fragment of the Armada fireback

A fireback made by Henry Neville of Mayfield

18

McDOUGALL'S FLOUR

It has been a distinctive landmark for many years to travellers using the A271 through Upper Horsebridge, north of Hailsham. Opposite the junction of London Road there stands, on the banks of the River Cuckmere, the remains of a fine water-driven flour mill that once belonged to McDougall's, producers of self-raising and plain flour.

Corn grinding water mills have existed here since before the 16th century, often worked by monks from nearby monasteries. In 1792 there was a move to construct a canal from Beddingham on the River Ouse to a newly built Horsebridge Mill to open up the area for better trading, but the idea never came to fruition.

It would appear that the mill was then twice destroyed by fire. An advertisement in the *Sussex Advertiser* of September 30, 1884 stated: 'To be sold by auction 1884, the site of Horsebridge Water and Steam Corn Mill. The property comprises the aforesaid remains of the well constructed mill, lately burnt out, including the walls and loose fallen bricks, the large waterwheel, nearly intact, shaft and large cog wheels in the mill, the 10hp horizontal

Entrance to Horsebridge Watermill as it is today

engine with double cylinder (by Clayton and Shuttleworth) just out of repair, a new 20hp boiler by W. H. Nicholson and Son of Newark on Trent, undamaged, the boiler house and shaft, in nearly perfect state. Also dwelling houses and land. The mill has recently been destroyed by fire and the owners and occupiers, being men advanced in years, are not practical millers, are desirous to leave the reconstruction to younger hands, and an opportunity is thus given to an energetic man to fit up a new building with modern machinery under his own superintendance.'

On January 2, 1908, when the property belonged to the Horsebridge Roller Milling Company, another fire gutted the building. The Old Hailsham Manual Pump was first on the scene, followed by the Eastbourne Steam Pump pulled by four horses.

McDougall's took over the mill in 1921 and spent a great deal of money on modernising the plant. Although the old breast wheel driven by the river was still used until the 1930s, the main driving power came from a steam engine which operated the dynamo generating electricity for light and power. In the Thirties an electric motor was installed to drive all the machines by main line shafts and belts. Later, in the mid-Forties, independent motor devices were added to the new equipment.

Much of the wheat milled here was bought from East Sussex growers although some came from Romania and Canada and, post war, France and Russia. Delivered in lorries and waggons, in sacks or bulk containers, the grain was tipped into an enclosed hopper and conveyed to a receiving separator for preliminary cleaning. From the wheat bins it was passed to the screenroom where second cleaning by seives and aspirators removed further debris and a washer disposed of the dirt. The wheat was gradually dried in a conditioner by passing through radiator heaters and then transferred to conditioning bins for twenty-four hours before being milled. One of the managers, a Mr Feneley, claimed he could tell when a storm was brewing some twenty-four hours beforehand because when the dried wheat was re-weighed it would vary from the norm.

Each grade of wheat was cleaned and conditioned separately then mixed to make up the 'grist' to give the right characteristics to the flour.

The wheat then went on the break system, which consisted of fluted rollers and centrifugal sieves. The rollers broke open the wheat, releasing the particles of semolina which were passed to purifiers to grade it by size and, by upward air current, remove the light pieces of wheat skin. Once purified, the semolina was passed to the gradual reduction system consisting of smooth rollers to crush into flour particles, these being sieved out by centrifugal force.

Afterwards the flour was passed, in closed conveyers, to the packaging department on the opposite side of the mill yard, where Sealtite automatic packing machines would fill up the familiar McDougall 3lb and 1lb flour bags, plus a few 112lb sacks for the bulk trade. A sample of flour was taken every hour and sent to London for testing for quality and purity. Every fourth bag of flour was test weighed by hand and the filled bags were packed in cardboard boxes erected in premises nearby. These were put on to pallets ready to be loaded on lorries for delivery locally. The output of Horsebridge Mill was small in comparison with the up-to-date mills of today, being some 200 tons a week.

The mill owners and managers lived on site at the big Mill House and the sixteen or so supervisors, millers, packers and office staff were all local people from the surrounding district. Harold Beeny was a management trainee for McDougall's in the early 1950s and remembers Horsebridge Mill with affection. Milling is in his blood, his great great grandfather being Edward Beeny (1802-1870) a farmer, baker and brickmaker who once owned the mill at the top of Windmill Hill near Herstmonceux.

Harold has never forgotten the time when his father, who was then a director of F Strickland, the Hailsham-based agricultural merchant, turned up with a parcel of wheat to sell and haggled for a favourable price. Once agreed father and son slapped hands to seal the deal. Harold's father began to laugh. When Harold asked why, his father said: 'This is the best day of my life. I bought this load of corn from your brother this morning for 22s 3d per cwt, sold it to you this afternoon for 22s 9d and made 6d a cwt on the deal.'

Harold recalled: 'The mill foreman in the years from the 40s to 60s was Fred Eves, a man of some character. The young trainees were the bane of his life. Tricks were played on him whenever possible and his ability to mis-pronounce words was famous. He ran the local cadet corps, of which he was very proud, and we would persuade him to show us how to carry out a drill routine with brooms over our shoulders. Brooms with which we should have been sweeping the floors. When he caught on to our delaying tactics he'd yell "Clean the floor up!"'.

'The mill ran on shifts twenty-four hours a day, 6am to 2pm; 2pm to 10pm; 10pm to 6am. At night one man oversaw the mill, a second the screen room and kept the boiler going. The outside was regularly repainted white to maintain a good appearance and the wheel, because of its historical value, was routinely maintained.

'In my training days at the mill, in the mid-Fifties, long before employers offered the luxuries of staff canteens, we had a mess room, a building of some age, which was situated behind the mill gardener's cottage, where employees could sup a dubious cup of tea whilst eating their food brought from home.

Horsebridge Mill. On the left, the old breast wheel worked by the Cuckmere

The mess room was run by an ageing lady called Maud who came to work on an equally aged tricycle. A dear old thing, she was teased unmercifully by the younger people who often let down the tyres of her tricycle.

'The saddest time for me was being involved in organising the closure of the mill in 1969 because it had become uneconomic. Many people I had worked with and learnt from I had to make redundant. My abiding memory of McDougall's Horsebridge Mill and its employees is of a happy environment with many characters.'

19

CIDER

The earliest reference to cider making in Sussex was in 1275, when a Richard de Clifford was accused of stealing an apple mill and press belonging to the widow of Georfrey de Basco of Pagham.

At that time making cider was very much a cottage industry. In the fourteenth century seventy-four parishes in the west of the county were producing cider, but there were only six in the east. Tithes of cider were paid to the church, and often they were substantial amounts.

In 1684 Richard Haines of Sullington took out a patent for 'An art or method of improving, preparing and meliorating cyder, so as to put the strength or goodness of two or three hogsheads of the liquor into one, and render the same much more wholesome and delightful'. The process he described was: 'Put one hogshead of cyder and some fruit juice into a copper still, and then

Merrydown's off-licence and gift shop, opened in 1957

put the same amount into your other hogshead and fill it up; stir it about well and keep it close stopt; except one day in ten or twenty let it lie open five or six hours. Within three months this will be as strong as the best French wines and as pleasing, although different in taste. Additional spirit and more sugar to please will make this cyder like canary, and one pint of good spirit added to a gallon of cyder will make it equal to Spanish wines.'

Cider making in the county had declined by the nineteenth century. The 1841 Census reveals that there were no commercial cider makers left in Sussex, although it was still being produced on a small scale by country folk and farmers for their own consumption.

It was just over 100 years later that commercial production of Sussex cider began again. Merrydown Wine of Horam, which has grown from a cottage industry to a multi-million pound company, was started in 1946 by Jack Ward, Ian Howie and John Kellond-Knight. The trio were childhood friends at Knockmaroon kindergarten school in Eastbourne in the 1920s, but had lost touch with each other.

Jack Ward left school and went to Trinity College, Cambridge, to read English, but ended up studying music at the Frankfurt Conservatorium. Perhaps it was here that the foundations of Merrydown were laid. With his fellow pupils, Jack often drank Apfelwein, a low alcohol, rather sour German cider. Some years later, during a spell in hospital, Jack read an article in *The Daily Telegraph* how to make wine from various flowers. Eager to discover whether he could produce something similar to those he had enjoyed in Germany, he set about gathering flowers from the gorse bushes growing on the South Downs whilst convalescing at his mother's Eastbourne home. It was winter and there was not much else available. Although he followed the recipe carefully, the fermentation stuck. The wine was undrinkable.

Impatient to know more Jack searched book shops and libraries and came across Peggy Hutchinson's *Home Made Wine Secrets*, which contained recipes for turning flowers, fruit and vegetables into alcohol. But again, his efforts, this time with potatoes, were unsuccessful.

The process of fermentation was an exact science and Jack did not know how to solve the problem. But luck, and a shilling, changed his life.

In Germany in 1938 he spotted a small paperback book in a shop window. The title was *Die Obst-und Beerenweinbereitung* (*The Preparation of Wine from Soft and Top Fruit*). For the equivalent value of one shilling Jack finally learnt about the vagaries of fermentation, the action of bacteria, sugar and acid readings, and which garden fruits made the best wines.

Back home he met Ian Howie, who also became intrigued, enthusiastic and eager to try out the possibilities of turning fruit into wine. Ian, a linguist, had various translation jobs before making a killing in gold mine speculation. With money from the sale of the shares he took himself off to South Africa to visit a distant cousin, where he made even more money – then lost the lot when the market crashed. He returned to England a poorer but wiser man and, during one of his periods of impoverishment, met Jack Ward again.

Both men were anxious to try wine making and they bought a quantity of Red Devon apples from a local farmer. Although Jack had a small drum press it was not up to mass production. It took all day to cut and press the apples which produced just ten gallons of juice. The liquid was poured into a glass carboy and dried wine yeast was added, plus potassium pyrosulphite to kill the wild yeasts. The vessel was stored in the conservatory of Ian Howie's house and left to ferment.

In 1939 Jack married Betty Ward and they bought a house near Rotherfield, called Merrydown. Jack took a job teaching music at a private school in Frant and to earn extra money during the holidays he worked as a travel courier in France and Switzerland. On his travels he acquired a superior soft fruit press of central screw type, ideal for making redcurrant wine.

With war threatening the tour guides were sent home. Jack caught a train to Dieppe and in the early hours of the morning arrived at Newhaven on the day war was declared. Turned down by the Royal Navy after a medical examination confirmed a heart complaint, Jack found work with a firm which collected postage stamps and was able to pursue his passion for making wine. He overcame the strict sugar rationing by swapping the family's chicken eggs for sugar.

Obtaining a supply of redcurrants from a farm at Shipbourne, near Sevenoaks, and using the newer press, Jack followed the instructions in his German book and made ten gallons of wine. While waiting for it to ferment he and Betty decided they would go and sample a bottle or two of the apple wine which had been left before the war to mature in Ian's conservatory.

On the journey home there was a loud popping noise. One of the bottles had blown its cork, throwing champagne cider around the car. Between Eastbourne and Rotherfield the five remaining bottles all blew. Jack drank the contents and, years later, commented: 'It was just a well there were no breathalyser tests in those days!'

The redcurrant wine, when ready for bottling, was excellent, so Jack then tried whitecurrants, which were equally successful.

In 1946, Ian Howie, recently demobbed from the Army, came visiting and after sampling some of Jack's wines he suggested they form a company to make redcurant wine and vintage cider.

On November 22, 1946, the inaugural meeting was held at Merrydown. Ian suggested they ask their friend John Kellond-Knight to join them. The three each put up £100 to finance their embryonic company which they named after Jack's cottage.

Doug Hoath of nearby Court Farm, loaned them a large 300 year old cider press which could turn out hundreds of gallons of juice in a short time. It was stored in the garage and Jack and Betty's baby Austin had to stand outside.

Sugar rationing was still in force. Ian, always game to try anything, managed to persuade the Ministry of Food to give them a permit for half a ton. The rest they begged, scrounged and traded with friends and neighbours for bottles of wine.

Jack, economically resourceful, utilised bits of an old Anderson shelter to make racking around the walls of the garage for the carboys of wine, leaving just enough room for the press to be operated.

The Customs and Excise at Tunbridge Wells had to be notified as the fruit juice was classified as British wine and carried a duty of 10/6p a gallon.

To extract fluid, the fruit had to be wrapped between pieces of hessian which served as press-cloths. Some ageing squares of sacking had been sent along with the cider press and bore the yellowing traces of apple juice from years before. The only container big enough in which to soak this somewhat unhygienic material was Jack's bath. But even when cleaned the remnants of the apple juice left in the press-cloths had such a bleaching effect that the next batch of redcurrant wine turned out a pale sickly pink colour.

The fermenting wine was stored in large carboys which Ian had unearthed in his travels around London. After that they had to seek out second hand bottles; new ones were unobtainable because of the shortage of raw materials. They chose hock bottles for the redcurrant wine, champagne bottles for the cider and rigged up a Heath Robinson bottle washing device consisting of two revolving brushes and a large tank of hot water, both of which constantly overloaded the electricity system and blew the fuses.

On holiday in Switzerland, Jack and Betty visited Wadenswil, where there was a research station doing work on various problems connected with wine, fruit and garden maintenance. A Dr Gerber provided useful advice, including that of using live wine yeast which would be active at lower temperatures and ideal for fermenting the vintage cider when the weather turned cold.

The trio bought a secondhand Nissen hut and installed it in Jack's garden to accommodate the carboys and bottles of wine.

In 1946 Ian Howie's father died and with his inheritance, for £3,500 he bought a corner property at Horam on the Eastbourne road. It consisted of an oast house which, when renovated, his mother could live in, plus a burnt out manor house and a piece of land. The plan was for Horam Manor to be leased out to the wine company, with an option to purchase.

With no money yet coming in from the sale of the wines, and the burnt out building needing a great deal of work done on it, the trio dipped into their pockets to put more money into the fledgling company. They were hit by a bitter blow when the Chancellor of the Exchequer, Stafford Cripps, virtually doubled the duty on all British wines in his 1947 Budget. As a result they decided to concentrate more on the vintage cider, which remained duty free.

They drove around Kent and Sussex occasionally going up to London, in an attempt to find buyers for their cider. In those early days it was a struggle trying to persuade people to try this new, and somewhat strong, cider but eventually the orders began flooding in.

Soon they were able to buy a new press and an elevator which would carry the crushed fruit up from a mill. In spite of the Budget they decided to produce a small quantity of redcurrant wine.

The Ministry of Food increased their allocation of sugar from half a ton to five tons.To supplement this, Ian Howie found a supply of Australian syrup, which had no adverse effect on the wine or cider. Another acceptable sugar based alternative was fondant, shipped in from Holland. The white blocks were packed in wooden crates and stored in a barn. One batch, when opened on the Monday after a weekend of blazing sunshine, was found to be greatly diminished as all the bees and wasps in the neighbourhood had been enjoying free lunches for two days.

By 1947 the first employee joined Merrydown, fifteen-year-old Maisie Stepney from Horsebridge, followed by part timer, seventeen-year-old Michael Heath, step-son of one of Ian Howie's brothers.

Everyone pitched in and lent a hand where it was needed. Spooning the sugar into the barrels and giving it a stir, loading up the old two ton laundry van with delivery orders, washing bottles, filling, corking and labelling them. There were assorted sacks, boxes and bags of apples to be carried to the press-house, hundred-weight sacks of sugar to be stored.

By 1950 they were in a position to employ a salesman, Dennis Carpmael, who was taken on at a wage of £400 per annum. Jack was now working full time in general production and maintenance, John had taken over sales and transport and Ian sales, packing, labelling and rail despatch. The lease of the refurbished Manor House was bought from the Howie family and promptly offered to Westminster Bank as part security for the business instead of Merrydown cottage.

Also in 1950 they made their first profit, £882. By 1956 the profit for an eighteen-month period had leapt to £82,965. That autumn they pressed 400,000 gallons of apple juice, a thousand fold increase on that first pressing.

Over the following years they were able to invest in new oak vats, a proper bottle cleaning machine, more presses, and a new plant for the production of vinegar. They bought a nearby property, The Grange, originally to use as another warehouse, but turned it into living quarters for young married members of their staff.

In 1955 John Kellond-Knight emigrated to Australia and his £80,000 stake in the company was sold.

In his 1956 Budget Harold Macmillan slapped a duty of 10/6d on a gallon of cider over 15% proof alcohol. Merrydown's was 17-18% proof and although some other competitors reduced the strength of their products to escape paying the duty, Jack and Ian wanted to keep their Vintage Cider unique. Faced with a two thirds cut in turnover, coupled with fast disappearing profits, they met the problem head on and increased the cider to 24% proof spirit. Although there had been a severe drop in sales at the beginning, turnover slowly picked up, allowing them to shelve the possibility of producing a cider below 15% proof.

But profit for the year 1956-57 was only £3,690, and trying to diversify and generate additional income, Jack suggested they added new varieties to the range of fruit wines, grow their own vines and develop the production of organic compost from the apple residue.

In the early days a couple of pigs kept at The Grange had been raised in part by the pomace, and Colonel White from Church Farm bought a herd of toothless ewes for a next-to-nothing price, fed them on the apple residue and was rewarded with a fine batch of very cheap spring lambs.

As demand once again grew for the cider they hit upon the idea of building a compost heap with the residue. The press cloths were thrown into a wheelbarrow, taken down to the heap and shaken out. As the pulp was piled on, the mound got higher and eventually solidified. Attempts to encourage it rot down by adding paper, cardboard and used sugar sacks proved unsuccessful.

Overrun with yet more waste from the press-house, several tons of untreated pomace was dumped under trees in the grounds of The Grange. As it became saturated with rain an anaerobic fermentation began, generating a dreadful smell that quickly had the neighbours complaining. Then all the trees died, overwhelmed by such a concentration of acid.

Eventually the problem was solved when, in the late 1950s, the company began turning out bags of Pompost, pure organic compost containing Merrydown's pomace combined with straw and chicken droppings from Buxted Chicken Company. But producing the compost was highly labour intensive and after a few years it started to lose money and was discontinued.

With vintage cider now dutiable the company actively tried to market its lesser known cider vinegar, called Martlet. Fanny and Johny Craddock recommended it in their television cookery programmes but sales took off in 1960 when a book called *Folk Medicine,* written by D C Jarvis, highlighted the properties of cider vinegar as an effective aid to slimming. The response was overwhelming. Usual monthly sales of Martlet were one hundred dozen bottles. This rocketed to ten thousand dozen bottles. And as *Folk Medicine* was translated into other languages, so exports went up.

Merrydown's next venture was mead, originally produced to use up a substantial supply of honey. At 9/9d a bottle, three hundred gallons were sold in the last two weeks of August 1963, when it first came on the market and sales doubled that in September. Merrydown had found another money spinner and by Christmas 1970 was being advertised as an alternative to sweet sherry.

Ian Howie's hard work for the company was recognised when he was awarded the MBE for his services to British exports.

Jack Ward continued to pursue his dream of growing vines. Since the early 1950s he had been experimenting in a two-acre vineyard, turning out Muller-Thurgau wine. In 1962 the land was sold to a property developer and Jack planted two new vineyards, half an acre at the Brickyard and half an acre at Horam Manor. In the Brickyard were 800 vines grafted on American root stock but because they had been planted too deep into solid, badly drained clay, on ground that sloped the wrong way to catch the sun, every plant died. At a second attempt Jack tried using rooted cuttings and liberal amounts of Pompost mixed into the clay. Not only did the plants grow, they thrived.

In 1969 The English Vineyards Association was formed with Jack ward as its chairman. Merrydown had introduced a co-operative scheme to bring together small growers who needed help to produce English wine. The yearly subscription

Ian Howie pictured in 1984 in front of the old cider press bought in 1954 from a local farmer. It is identical to that borrowed in 1946 for the first pressing of Merrydown Vintage Cider

Jack Ward pictured grape picking in his vineyard in 1978

was £1, and the ten original members had a combined fifteen acres of vines.

Growers could pay Merrydown in cash or kind (part of the juice) to have their wine made. The company even made half a dozen bottles for Princess Margaret from her Kensington Palace grapes. In 1976 180 tons of grapes were processed but gradually, as more small growers began to look after their own interests, and Merrydown was having to cope with a booming vintage cider market, it reluctantly had to pull out of the scheme. Jack was consoled that Kenneth McAlpine, owner of Lamberhurst Vineyards, bought The Brickyard vinery as a going concern.

With more Budget increases on the duty on wine and sales again falling, Jack and Ian decided the company needed a thorough and professional overhaul. In 1971 they called in a firm of management consultants who produced a business plan.

The company's expensive apple press often stood idle, and during such periods it was arranged for Merrydown to process hundreds of thousands of gallons of fruit for other manufacturers. Merrydown expanded further by taking on contract bottling. Huge tankers brought in bulk loads of wine and the company bottled and labelled some quarter million cases of wine a year.

When Excise duty went through the roof, the firm reluctantly decided to produce a new Vintage Cider under 15% proof. Due to a slight malfunction during production, there was a small problem of secondary fermentation causing a number of bottles to explode. It is said that the sales force went equipped with motorcycle crash helmets, goggles and gauntlets to retrieve bottles blowing up like bombs in supermarkets and off-licences.

It did not appear to do the business any harm, in fact Merrydown became the fourth largest cider maker in Britain and found a big following in the north. The company entered the Unlisted Securities Market in January 1981. By the mid 1980s profits had risen to over a million pounds. Ten years later Merrydown was worth £5 million.

20

POTTERY

Pottery has been made in this county since before the time of the Roman invasion. The most distinctive and best remembered is probably the brown earthenware Sussex Pig.

Such was the popularity of this plump and well-conditioned animal that it was turned out in large quantities and could be seen in nearly every rural home in the area. Pigs appeared in the late 18th century alongside the emergence of identifiable Sussex ware and were such a characteristic of the county that it was jokingly suggested they could be adopted as the county coat of arms with, beneath, well known Sussex saying 'We wun't be druv'.

> *And you can pook*
> *And you can shuv*
> *But a Sussex pig*
> *He wun't be druv.*

The pigs were actually drinking vessels and often made appearances at festive occasions when the liquid, usually beer, was poured from the pig's body into the detachable head which served as the cup. Drinkers could then claim they had drunk a 'whole hogshead'.

Older specimens of the brown, and sometimes black, glazed pigs are now extremely rare. Frederick Mitchell, of Rye Pottery, revived the production of Sussex pigs around the late 1860s. His were of a light biscuit colour brought about by the mixing of paler Dorset clays with the rich red Sussex clays.

Until the late 18th century pottery made in Sussex had no particular identifying characteristics. Traces of Roman pottery have been found in Sussex. Excavations at Lewes in 1846 revealed a crude representation of a man on horseback and in 1858, at Seaford, a similar piece of pottery was found. Both were containers for liquid and are credited to a twelfth century Hastings pottery.

At Horsham, in 1867, a number of thirteenth century jugs and pitchers were found, along with an iron tool used for their ornamentation.

From the late 18th century lead glazed brown Sussex pottery came into its own, the rich colour derived from the iron in Wealden clay which was in superabundance in the eastern region.

The first dated piece is a large two-handled cider jar which has 'John Robinson 1707'on the front. A 1777 catalogue of the the wares of Samuel Drawbridge, a potter from Nutley, contained` the first direct reference to items of Sussex Pottery.

Potters could set up business almost anywhere in Sussex as long as there was suitable good clay, an abundance of wood to fire the kilns and a nearby stream. A rental was paid for the use of the land and often a licence or permission had to be sought, and paid for, to dig out the clay.

Much of the pottery was unglazed and initially made to satisfy a local need for utilitarian items such as flower pots, bricks, tiles, animal feeding bowls and drainage pipes. Glazed ware was more likely to be used inside the home. They included butter churns, chamber pots, candlesticks, crockery with lids for storing food, drinking vessels and multi-chambered money boxes.

Cider jar incised 'John Robinson 1701' in dark brown glaze

The clay was dug out of the ground with a pick and shovel in the autumn and left for the winter frosts to break down the soil. In the spring it would be puddled with water to make it more malleable before being shovelled into a pug mill. This was a circular drum with an upright centre spindle with attached blades that, when turned, would chop and mix the clay which was then extruded from the base of the drum. Power came originally from a horse harnessed to a horizontal bar at right angles to the central spindle. Later this job was taken over by a small steam engine.

The clay was then heaped up and covered with old sacking until it was needed. Chunks were taken out and carefully inspected for bits of grit and small stones before being rolled into balls ready for use.

Experienced spinners would know exactly how big a ball was needed to throw on the potter's wheel to make any particular item. The ware would then be placed on racks and left until partly dry when handles and other decorations were added before firing.

Food or water receptacles needed to be glazed. This consisted of a highly poisonous powdered lead which was applied with the fingers or mixed with a clay slip of creamy consistency and painted on. Glazing added to the richness of colour after firing.

The wares were then placed in a kiln by men known as crowders. Firing to a temperature of around 1000°C produced the rich dark brown finish. The kiln would take three to five days to reach the required heat. A trial pot, hooked out by means of a metal pole, would indicate how the firing was progressing. Once finished, the fires were extinguished and the kiln left to cool for about a week before the wares were removed.

Many potteries were little more than family businesses, run to satisfy local needs. By the end of the 19th century Sussex potteries were in a decline brought about by competition from coke-fired Midland potteries which were mass producing cheaper, lighter, whiter wares, and using the rail system to transport them all over the country. The wood fuel for the kilns was becoming difficult to get and the use of poisonous, but cheap, lead glazes was restricted by Board of Trade regulations.

The potteries that survived turned to producing unglazed items, flowerpots provided the mainstay of some, others specialised in 'fancy-ware'.

Among Sussex potteries with interesting histories are the following.

RYE

The first of the Rye potteries to become well established was at Cadborough, a substantial farm owned at the end of the 18th century by lime burner and brickmaker James Smith. In 1809 he advertised:

> Wanted one or two good hands as Spinners,
> who can have constant employment. For particulars
> enquire at Messrs. Smith and Collet's Kiln, Rye, Sussex.

He was succeeded by his son Jerimiah (1794-1864) 'a brickmaker, lime burner and potter' who, apart from managing some of the largest hop gardens in England as well as being one of the biggest flock-masters in Sussex, supervised the workings of the pottery. One of the employees at Cadborough was a William Mitchell (1793-1871) from High Halden,

Flagon with flattened sides, made at Rye Pottery, June 1845

91

in Kent. This was an area well known for its pottery and he could have receiving his training there before moving to Hellingly and then possibly to Dicker before going to Rye to manage the Cadborough works. In 1834 he advertised for another potter:

Wanted immediately a brown ware potter that perfectly
understands the Making in all its branches, can have
Constant Employ; a single man will be preferred. Apply to
Wm. Mitchell, at Mr. Jerimiah Smith's Pottery, Rye,
Sussex. All letters post paid.

It would appear that Mitchell started the practise of marking 'Rye Pottery' and including the date on his wares. As the business grew, many of the products were distributed by way of the town harbour to other ports along the south coast.

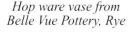

Mitchell experimented with mixing the local red clay with other clays brought in from outside the county, producing pieces far removed from the traditional Sussex ware. His son Frederick (1819-1875) turned his hand to decorating items with fruits, leaves and flowers.

In 1851 the Mitchells obtained a contract from the Hastings Commissioners to supply 'Earthen and Drain Pipes' for the new Ecclesbourne Valley water works and in 1866 they were described as 'Manufacturers to HRH The Prince of Wales and the Queen of Spain of the celebrated brown and rustic fancy ware'.

Hop ware vase from Belle Vue Pottery, Rye

Frederick Mitchell set up on his own in 1868, buying a seventy-five year lease on land at nearby Ferry Road, Rye, which became known as Belle View Pottery. He continued making his particular rustic ware, much of it containing somewhat excessive amounts of embellishments, especially of trailing hop vines, and he re-introduced the Sussex pig, albeit of a much paler colour.

William continued at Cadborough, helped by his other son Henry, until he died in 1871. Henry carried on, diversifying into more profitable brick and tile making, eventually selling out to a George Russell who carried on the business until about 1890.

At Belle View, Caroline Mitchell took over the business on the death of Frederick in 1875 and concentrated on producing copies of historical pieces, helped by her nephew Frederick Thomas Mitchell (1864-1920). When Caroline died he, having been trained as a watchmaker, found pottery production a challenge and experimented constantly for improvements, whilst continuing to produce pieces heavily decorated with leaves, hops, snakes and lizards. Items from these two Rye potteries may be seen in a number of Sussex museums.

BREDE

Potters and brick makers were active in the area from around the fourteenth and fifteenth centuries. Henry Richardson may have started the Brede pottery works in the mid 1700s. In his will of February 5, 1796 he left:

> *'...messuages, tenements, gardens, brick kilns, tile kilns, pot kiln buildings and a piece of land whence or near to which the said Buildings are standing and works are carried on, containing by estimation 6 acres...'*

His son Henry was also bequeathed the adjacent 100-acre Great Park Wood on the understanding that 'owners or occupiers for the time being of my pot kiln, brick kilns and tile kilns have the liberty of digging and taking therefrom Clay and earth for the making of pots, bricks, tiles and suchlike ware as hereinafter mentioned'.

Two of the tenants were John and Thomas Rummons, and that name, in slightly different forms, occurs a number of times in connection with Brede pottery. An Edward Rumens may have been the originator of the attractive semi-circular, interlacing star decorated ware which was to be copied by a number of other potteries.

The cessation of this stylish form of decoration at Brede early in the 19th century proved to be a puzzle as no death of an Edward Rumens had been recorded in the local parish register. But in May 1809 an advertisement in the *Sussex Weekly Advertiser* provided a possible answer:

> *Whereas Edward Rummings of the Parish of Brede in the*
> *county of Sussex potter was balloted to serve in the*
> *Local Militia for the said parish of Brede, and has*
> *left the same without being enrolled or paying any penalty.*
> *NOTICE is hereby given, that if any person or persons*
> *will give information to the Churchwardens or*
> *Overseers of the said parish of Brede that he may be*
> *apprehended, shall be handsomely rewarded for their*
> *trouble. The said Edward Rummings is supposed to have*
> *a woman with him, of stout stature. Rummings is about*
> *5 feet 8 inches high, rather of a light complexion,*
> *full eyed, brown hair, and is supposed to be working*
> *in the neighbourhood of Ditchling in Sussex.*

History has not recorded what eventually happened to Edward Rumens. Another family name connected to Brede pottery is that of Weller. In 1797 a

93

Thomas Weller married Mary Rumens and the union produced four sons and two daughters, all but one of whom migrated to the United States. John stayed behind and helped his father with the business. He married Mary Barnes in 1826.

The Wellers had a natural aptitude for pottery, aided by 'potters' fingers' – short and practical – and John had a theory that one way to avoid lead poisoning whilst applying glaze was to chew plenty of orange peel. Many craftsmen tried to discover why the Weller glaze did not appear to crack and one of the ingredients of this closely guarded secret turned out to be human urine.

The marriage of John and Mary produced eight sons and four daughters. Albert the eldest (b1827), helped in the family business until about 1850 before moving to a pottery at High Halden in Kent. Thomas (b1842) went to potteries at Bethersden, Enoch (b1834) occasionally assisted with the business as did Edward (b1841), but spent most of his time working at Church House Farm. Luke (b1844) was the delivery man, in charge of the horse and cart, carrying the wares, carefully packed in straw, all around the neighbouring villages, as far away as Goudhurst. John (b1840) died at sixteen of a fever and the youngest, James (b1849), preferred horses to pottery and left the area. Aaron (b1830) carried on the family tradition with his father and was recognised as being a fine spinner. His eyesight began to fail in later life and his pots became crooked.

Additional assistance came from travelling potters who would pass through and stay for a few months. One, Irving Hall, always wore clothes that were far too long and he was affectionately called Shufflebreeches. Another was Adam Switzer ,who was fascinated by astronomy and spiritualism, and travelled around finding work with Sussex brick, tile or pottery makers during the summer, spending the winter in the workhouse.

A specialty of the Brede works in the late nineteenth century were hand-made hedgehog ornaments, and Knocker Weller, Aaron's son, took pleasure in making pottery hens with chicks as well as producing some realistic looking snakes. Whistling birds were also made at Brede. These were pottery models with whistles in their tails, which were built into some local farmhouse chimneys. When the wind blew the birds whistled and were believed to keep evil spirits away. The pottery was also responsible for

A Brede hedgehog

making The Brede Ogre, a wall plaque purporting to represent Sir Goddard Oxenbridge, who, it was rumoured, ate little children. Legend says that he returned from market one day and, being a little the worse for drink, fell asleep by the roadside and was sawn in half with a wooden saw by a band of Kent and Sussex children.

When Aaron Weller died in 1892 the business was already in decline due to a shortage of suitable clay. Many of the pieces remaining at the pottery were sold to Hastings Museum.

DICKER

Like many of the other potteries Dicker, in the parish of Hellingly, near Hailsham, evolved on land that had been used for this purpose at least since medieval times, when it may have had a connection to nearby Michelham Priory.

Apart from its specialties, Brown 'treacleware' and 'Sussex Iron or Pewter Glaze', which produced an unusual metallic lustre, the pottery at Dicker, then sited alongside Coldharbour Lane, is probably best remembered for the acrimonious squabbling between Thomas Wood and William Cuckney in 1774-75. The first round was fired on December 19, 1774 when the following advertisement appeared in the *Sussex Weekly Advertiser*:

> *This is to acquaint my Friends and the Public that*
> *the business of making Crockery Ware at that kiln in*
> *the Dicker, in Hellingly, late in partnership with*
> *WILLIAM CUCKNEY is now carried on solely by me,*
> *having provided a Workman whose skill in that branch*
> *has made some improvements.*
> *Those who please to favour me with their Commands may*
> *depend on the utmost Dispatch of their Orders and*
> *being furnished with the neatest Goods by Their*
> *obliged humble servant,*
> *THOMAS WOOD, HELLINGLY, Dec. 19. 1774.*
> *P.S. Likewise the BRICK and TILE TRADE carried on by*
> *the same THOMAS WOOD, that Gentlemen, or others, may*
> *be supplied with Earthen Pipes, for Drains, or Bar*
> *Places, at reasonable prices.*

In the January 23, 1775 issue of the same newspaper William Cuckney responded in similar fashion:

> *An Advertisement having lately appeared in this paper*
> *signed THOMAS WOOD, seemingly calculated to mis-*
> *inform the Public, that I had declined the Business*

of making CROCKERY. I therefore hereby inform the
Public, that I have now finished an entire new KILN
on the DICKER (near the old one, which DID belong to
THOMAS WOOD) and am provided with the Workmen from
the old KILN, whose Ware at all times has and will
attest which has the most skill in making, glazing
and burning CROCKERY.
Those who please to favour me with their Commands,
may depend on my best Endeavours to serve them, so as
to merit future Favours; and am, Their obliged humble
servant, WILLIAM CUCKNEY, Hellingly, Jan 16. 1775.

Thomas Wood put in another advertisement on February 6, defending his previous statements. The situation was somewhat ironic as both businesses were small and each employed only one potter.

By early 1776 Thomas Wood had become a bankrupt and in May his Dicker brickmaking and pottery business was put up for auction at the King's Head, Horsebridge, and was bought by Thomas and James Peckham, who concentrated on the brickyard, only to sell it on a year later to an Edward Goldsmith, who appears to have specialised in brown earthenware pottery and flowerpots. There still seems to have been some sniping from the other pottery as a notice was issued stating:

Iron lustre glaze pots made at Dicker Pottery between 1920 and 1940

N.B. The Public are desired to take notice that the
malicious Report of the ware's not being good, is
without any foundation, as they who spread it never
saw the Goods, tho' they have often been asked to
come and view them.

Edward Goldsmith died in 1781 and other members of the family continued to run the business whilst trying to sell it as a going concern. The Mitchell family, who were mentioned at the Cadborough Pottery, Rye, were tenants here, and in 1809, advertised for two journeymen potters 'who understood the business in all its branches, one to make only and the other to burn and make occasionally'.

The 1851 Census returns listed a 'Boship Pottery' on the north side of the Lewes Road, which had been in the hands of the Miller family since 1821. The Millers, who made 'red and white chimney, pots, socket pipes and junctions, slate red ridge and hip tiles, flower pots and vases, wash pans and bowls, ceased trading in 1890 and their skilled potter, Benjamin William Henry Bridger, went across the road to work for Uriah Clark.

What became known as The Dicker Pottery was just a brickyard when bought by the Clark family in 1845. Uriah Clark, 'a brown ware potter' had his fingers in a lot of pies. He had originally hawked wares from door to door with a pony and cart and in various trade directories was described as a 'coal and coke merchant, grocer, draper and blacksmith'. He developed the business into a pottery and when he died in 1903, aged ninety-six, he was said to be worth £30,000. After his death the pottery became known as Uriah Clark and Nephew.

By the 1920s The Dicker Pottery had twenty employees aged from twelve upwards, including four shop staff, labourers to dig the clay from thirteen acres of ground and two office staff, most working fifty hours a week. Visitors to the factory could see all the wares – more than 200 different items, including reproductions of Roman and early English vases, bowls, jugs and candlesticks – being hand made. Publicity leaflets put forward the idea that Dicker Pottery was an ideal place to see on a country run in the car. (See also Appendix 5).

Vase with painted slip decoration, dated 1774, believed to have been made at potteries on the Dicker

During the Second World War the Army requisitioned the buildings. The premises were re-built in 1948 and taken over by the Dick Whittington, Mayor of Lewes, who put in a manager of little experience. By 1958 the Dicker Pottery was no more. The last employee to leave was Francis Robb, a skilled thrower who had had been at the Dicker since 1919. He recalled the time in 1920 when film producer Duncan McRae, using some of the potters as extras and paying them half a crown, made a film at the pottery called *Burnt In,* a murder mystery. At the end, he said, the original kilns, a bottle shaped up-draught and a round down-draught, had become so unsafe that anyone passing by them had to whisper so as not to cause them to collapse. When the Dicker Pottery ceased trading Kerridges of Hailsham bought all the stock.

Francis Robb moved on to Brickhurst Pottery at Laughton, which had been opened in August 1952 by Keith and Fiona Richardson, who carried on the Dicker tradition of lustrous black glaze.

Fiona Richardson had worked at the Dicker Pottery from 1946, helping to set it up again after the war. She left after a year and later set up Brickhurst Pottery with her husband Keith. The Richardsons ceased commercial trading in 1982, but are still making jugs and bowls as a hobby.

Another Dicker employee, Norman Benjamin Bridges, joined the Richardsons at Laughton in 1956. He left in 1963 to start his own pottery business, called Merlin, at Hellingly. He retired in the 1970s.

CHAILEY

At Chailey, as at Dicker, there were two rival potteries, the Allchorn Pottery and the Chailey Pottery which was in the Norman family hands for 150 years. Here there seems to have been a trend to include verse on punch bowls, flasks, tobacco canisters and barrels such as:

> *THOUGH WE AT CHAILEY ARE BUT MEAN*
> *WE DO THE THINGS THAT'S NEAT AND CLEAN*
> *FILL YOUR GLASSES LADS AND LASSES*
> *ROUND THE MAYPOLE FRISK AND PLAY*
> *SMILING GLANCING SINGING DANCING*
> *THIS IS CUPID'S HOLIDAY*
> *MY TOBACCO I DO PUT*
> *WITHIN THIS LITTLE POT*
> *AND MY FRIEND MAY HAVE A PIPE*
> *IF ANY I HAVE GOT*

Another specialty was a portable round spirit flask with a clock face on one side and a verse around the edge.

During the 1930s Heals, the London department store, bought quantities of traditional brown Sussex ware from the Chailey potteries, but the works closed in 1939 due to the war and when they re-opened afterwards only bricks were made. The business was bought out in 1959 by the Redland Brick Company.

Spirit flask made by Richard Russell of Chailey in 1839

DITCHLING and BURGESS HILL

Ditchling Common pottery was famed for its terracotta and Burgess Hill (formerly known as St John's Common) pottery was owned by the Chailey Norman family at the beginning of the nineteenth century. In 1870 owners

William and Frederick Meeds were turning out a variety of wares including miniature pieces alongside mole and sparrow traps at the Burgess Hill pottery. By mixing lighter Staffordshire clays with the red Sussex clay they also produced some variegated pottery.

JCJ POTTERY

Jonathan Chiswell Jones, representative of many contemporary Sussex potters, works from converted stables at Peelings Manor Barn, Stone Cross. A teacher of English, he said that the turning point in his life came when, as he was dabbling in the school's art room, up to his elbows in a bucket of glaze, a pupil said: 'Sir, wouldn't you rather be doing that than teaching us English?' Jonathan agreed and did a one-year course at Farnham Art School followed by eight months with Scottish potter Joe Finch.

Originally he set up in business at Drusillas Zoo Park, Alfriston, and in 1998, he moved to the present site. The clay he uses today is no longer local. 'The Sussex clay belongs to a period of history and we've moved on since then,' he says. He uses a porcelain clay from Cornwall that can be fired to a temperature of 1260°C, which would melt local clay, but is ideal for tableware and is capable of taking a glaze that doesn't craze.

Pottery by Jonathan Chiswell Jones

His potter's wheel is electrically driven, but all the old skills are still needed to turn out good pots. His biggest kiln he made from high temperature insulation fire bricks backed up by a wrap of ceramic fibre sandwiched between metal mesh.

Firing takes place about once a month when the wares are stacked carefully on a variety of adjustable shelves so they will not touch each other and fuse together. A gentle warmth is introduced by Calor gas heating which, overnight, brings the temperature up to 100°C. Early the following morning, by changing over to oil heating, the temperature climbs to 1260°C which is maintained for some fourteen hours. Two days later the now cooled ware is taken out, inspected and the bases rubbed smooth.

21

NEEDLES

At the beginning of the seventeenth century the suburb of St Pancras in Chichester was one of the important centres in England for the manufacture of fine quality needles – made from Wealden metal. Although there were some fourteen manufacturers listed in the seventeenth century there is no record of when this cottage industry first became established here – yet as early as the twelfth century there were families living in the area with the names of Nedeler or Nedler. Alexander Hay, in his *History of Chichester* (1804), speculates that the people of the area first learned to make crude metal needles from the Romans and that, under their protection and encouragement, raised the trade to some eminence.

In the Siege of Chichester in 1642, during the Civil War, much of St Pancras – which was outside the city walls – was razed the ground by the Parliamentarians. The needle industry, then at its height, received a blow from which it never fully recovered.

One survivor, though, was a Robert Hichcock, who in 1667 issued a halfpenny token bearing the arms of the needle makers. Another, Isaac Hammond, made his mark, not by his trade, but by the discovery, in 1705, that he was cohabiting with a widow, Ann Deane, passing her off as his wife when he was still married with children. In his will of 1733 he left a six room house valued at £205 and his trade stock of 12,500 quilting needles, 35,000 large worsted needles, 65,000 large needles, 168,000 small needles, 221,000 assorted partly finished needles. These were valued at sixpence for quilting needles and two shillings and sixpence for large needles.

Increasing competition from the manufacturing towns in the north, which were producing cheaper, although inferior needles, began to bring about the demise of needle-making in the south. Master needle-makers employing apprentices and journeymen were forced to lay off their workers and by the end of the eighteenth century this industry had become extinct in the south.

22

HEATHFIELD NATURAL GAS

In 1896 natural gas was found at Heathfield railway station. Steam engines belonging to the London Brighton and South Coast Railway consumed generous quantities of water as they travelled on the hilly Eastbourne to Tunbridge Wells line, and often needed to take on more at Heathfield. Although a sump at the north end of the down platform was seventy-three feet deep, the amount of water collected was often inadequate. The company decided to drill down to 312 feet in the search for more water, but all that came out of the six inch wide bore hold was a bad smell.

Legend says that an onlooker lit his pipe and as he tossed away the lighted match a great ball of flame, sixteen feet high, erupted as escaping gas ignited. Numerous damp cloths placed over the tube mouth eventually extinguished the flames.

Once harnessed, the gas pressure was so great – at 140psi – that initial efforts to utilise this source of light resulted in ordinary incandescent mantles being blown to pieces. Fishtail burners were more successful and soon the railway station and many houses in the area were being lit by this ninety-six per cent pure methane natural gas. Surplus gas was collected each morning by a 'gasman' who arrived on a train from Tunbridge Wells with a truckload of cylinders to fill. The gas was then sold all over the country.

Expectations that there was a commercially viable gas field in Sussex prompted the formation of The Natural Gas Fields of England Ltd in 1902, with £70,000 to exploit it. The same year a coin was struck to record the duel events of King Edward's Coronation, and the first harnessing of natural gas for power and light. Copies made in a light white metal, with the words on the reverse side 'Natural Gas carried me from Heathfield, Sussex' were attached to balloons and

101

sent up on Coronation Day, August 9. A day later a balloon was picked up near Ulm in Wurtemburg, having travelled 600 miles in twenty-four hours.

There were dreams of Heathfield becoming another Pittsburgh, where hundreds of factories and thousands of dwellings were supplied by local natural gas. The boring of holes, one down to 400 feet, was carried on day and night, the gas supplying both the light and the power for the work.

The output grew to fifteen million cubic feet a day, and in the deepest hole the pressure was an impressive 200psi. More houses in Heathfield began to use this local gas and by 1903 more bore holes were being dug around the town in the hope of finding yet more supplies. There was talk of reviving the Sussex iron industry using this natural gas, bringing more employment and prosperity to the county. But the supply of gas did not keep pace with the dreams. The Natural Gas Fields of England Ltd made just £200 profit in 1903 and pulled out in 1904, as did two other speculators between then and 1910.

Nearby houses continued to be lit by gas until 1930, when they were converted to electricity, and the diminishing amounts of remaining gas were packed into cylinders and sold for experimental purposes to the Safety in Mines Research Board.

British Petroleum attempted some investigative boring in 1955, and Esso in 1963, but the gas field had been almost depleted. By 1965 the gas at Heathfield station had gone, and so had the trains.

Between the tunnel and the road bridge near Heathfield Station.
Beyond the water tower are two gasholders, which expanded
upwards as they were filled with natural gas from the bore hole

23

BEXHILL COAL

In 1804 a seam of what was thought to be coal was discovered at Bexhill. It was found by the surveyor of a company digging wells to obtain water supplies for the 5-6,000 troops of the King's German Legion, which had been brought in to help erect Martello towers.

A company was set up, but the coal, at the bottom of the Downs, near the present Ashdown Road, turned out to be only bands of lignite, formed from driftwood. The project was abandoned and surface buildings and mine workings were demolished in 1846, when the railway was being built.

In *Discourse on the Study of Natural Philosophy,* Sir John Herschell wrote: 'Not many years since an attempt was made to establish a colliery at Bexhill in Sussex. The appearance of thin sheets and seams of fossil wood, and wood coal, with some other indications similar to what occur in the neighbourhood of the great coal beds of the North of England, having led to the sinking of a shaft and the erection of machinery on a scale of vast expense. Not less than £80,000 are said to have been laid out on this project which, it is almost needless to add, proved completely abortive, as every geologist would have, at once, declared it must; the whole assemblage of geological facts being adverse to the existence of a regular coal bed in the Hastings strata. While this on which Bexhill is situated is separated from the coal measures by a series of interposed beds of such enormous thickness as to render all idea of penetrating through them absurd. The history of mining operations is full of similar cases where a very moderate acquaintance with the usual order of nature, to say nothing of the theoretical views, would have saved many a sanguine adventurer from utter ruin.'

In the 1920s labourers working in a brickfield at Chiddingly came upon some 'dirty brown coloured coal which, when put on a fire, burnt well'. Similar deposits have also been found at Heathfield. Surveyor Sylvan Harmer, in the *Brighton Guardian* in 1830, wrote: 'The land around Heathfield is replete with copious signs of coal mines, and about twenty years ago on the western side of the parish was discovered a strata of coal 10fi inches thick. Certain mineralogists from Derbyshire came to explore the same and gave very favourable reports, although no effort therein was resorted to.'

Veins of lignite run erratically through the Weald, lumps of it have even been found on Brighton beach.

24

OTHER CRAFTS AND INDUSTRIES

Listed here are some of the other items made or processed in Sussex over the centuries, and the names of well-known county companies, for which there is no space in this book. There are more than enough for *Made in Sussex Two*. I would be pleased to consider any information readers have on these, or any other Sussex crafts, companies or industries, and may be contacted via: SB Publications, 19 Grove Road, Seaford, East Sussex BN25 1TP.

Crafts and industries

Silk weaving at Buxted.
Bavin making
Sussex marble
Oyster picking at Newhaven
Flint picking at Eastbourne
Charcoal burning
Clay pipe making
Bell founding
Wattle making
Textiles

Tanning
Salt making
Horsham slate
Lime making
Ship building
Chicken fattening
Hay case making
Flax making
Gypsum mining
Gunpowder

Companies

Shippams Paste Company, Chichester. Dolphin Soap works (J Evershed), Kingston. Parker Pen Company, Newhaven. Judges Postcards, Hastings. Eastwoods Cement, Lewes. Lancaster Car Company. The Fryco Company, Brighton. Marlow Rope Company, Hailsham. Green's Sponges, Brighton.

ABOUT THE AUTHOR

Elizabeth Wright was educated at Kent College, Tunbridge Wells, and St Helena's-West Hill, Eastbourne. For thirty-eight years she managed a successful pet and garden centre in Eastbourne – and contributed articles about popular pets to such magazines as *Cage and Aviary Birds, Birds Illustrated* and *American Cage Bird Magazine*.

In 1992 Elizabeth decided to fulfil a lifelong ambition to become a full-time writer. Her work has since appeared in many other publications.

Made in Sussex is her first published book. She is now working on *Made in Sussex Two*, as well as a humourous novel based on her life, and a six-part television situation-comedy.

Elizabeth lives in Eastbourne with her teenage daughter and Joey, a talkative African Grey Parrot.

CRICKET BAT MANUFACTURE

The main materials used in making a cricket bat are willow and cane; willow for the blade because it is resilient, tough and light (no satisfactory substitute has been found) and cane for the handle because it is light and resilient. Other materials used are rubber, string or tape and glue: rubber (and sometimes cork) is used in the handle for the insertions known as springs, which absorb the jar and string or tape to bind the cane in the handles together - covered finally with a rubber grip.

The Cricket Bat Willow Cricket bat willows are grown from cuttings which are known in the trade as setts. They must be perfectly straight and free from knots and blemishes. When ready for planting the sett is some 12' high and can be either rooted or a straight cutting with no roots. For many years it has been a debatable point which produces the best results. The unrooted sett has the advantage of being easier to plant. Setts are planted 2' 6" into the ground and nearly 10' of the tree is kept free from branches and uses for cricket bats. In plantation form the setts should be planted in rows not less than 30' apart as they need plenty of light and air. In the first years of growth they must be protected from rabbits (and later cattle), shoots and buds must be kept rubbed off from the trunk to a height of 10'. Willow is an extremely fast growing timber and some years ago a tree was cut in Robertsbridge which measured 50" in circumference 5' from the ground after only nine years growth. A well grown willow tree after 12 years produces very valuable timber and under the right conditions is extremely profitable to grow.

There are a great many varieties of willow trees but few are suitable for bat making. The finest willow for cricket bats is known as Salix Alba Caerulea, a shapely tree, occasionally reaching a height of 100' and 15' to 18' girth. A willow tree is large enough for bat making when it reaches a circumference of 50" when measured 5' from the ground. Its height will then be somewhere around 40'. The timber of this variety is distinguished by a bright orange stain which is known in the trade as 'butterfly' stain. When these stains appear on the blades of bats players often reject them thinking that the stains are faults or knots, whereas they are in fact the hallmark of the finest quality cricket bat willow.

MANUFACTURE

Fell After the tree has been felled the trunk is cut into lengths of 2'4" which are then split with the grain by means of wooden wedges into sections known as clefts. Each cleft makes one cricket bat blade.

Seasoning As soon as possible after splitting the clefts are sawn into very roughly shaped cricket bat blades which are graded and stacked in the drying yards for seasoning which takes some 9-12 months. After seasoning, the blades are cut down to the correct width and the faces and backs are roughly shaped.

Pressing Each blade is pressed three times during the course of manufacture and the edges are also subjected to heavy pressure. This process is a most essential one, otherwise they would not stand up to the impact of a cricket ball.

Splice Cutting and Fitting handles Special machines are used to cut the splice in the blade and to cut the handles correspondingly wedge-shaped to fit. The handle is held in position only by means of glue and a perfect fit, the latter being essential because if the handle is too loose it will come out, and if too tight, the blade will split.

Handle Making Cricket bat handles are made from cane. The best cane is grown in the East Indies and is known as Manau. This is usually between 14 and 18mm in diameter and is sawn into the correct lengths for handles. It is then carefully sorted and graded to ensure that only absolutely sound pieces are used. These pieces of cane are then put through a cane splitting machine which planes them up on either side, so that they can be glued together. The handle is made up of 12-16 pieces of cane and rubber or cork insertions are used to absorb the jar. The handle is then turned to the correct shape, one end being cut wedge-shaped to fit into the blade.

Finishing (shaping) The final shaping of the bat is a highly skilled job and is done by means of drawknife, spoke-shave and plane, the greatest care being taken to obtain the correct balance and shape. After the blade has been shaped it is sanded on a sanding machine and then burnished on another machine which leaves the blade smooth and glossy.

Gripping of Handles After sanding the bat is rotated in a lathe while the handle is bound with tape and string. (This is why there is a little whole in the bottom of the blade - the bat is pushed onto a spike to hold it in position while it is being rotated. This hole is often incorrectly referred to as an 'oil-hole'). The rubber grip is then applied.

Grading During the course of manufacture blades and handles are continually inspected for defects and the finished bats is finally sorted into the various grades ready for selection according to the customers' special requirements.

Branding Before the bats are dispatched from the factory they are branded with the maker's name and the label cosmetics.

The author and publisher thank Gray Nicholl's of Robertsbridge for kindly supplying this information.

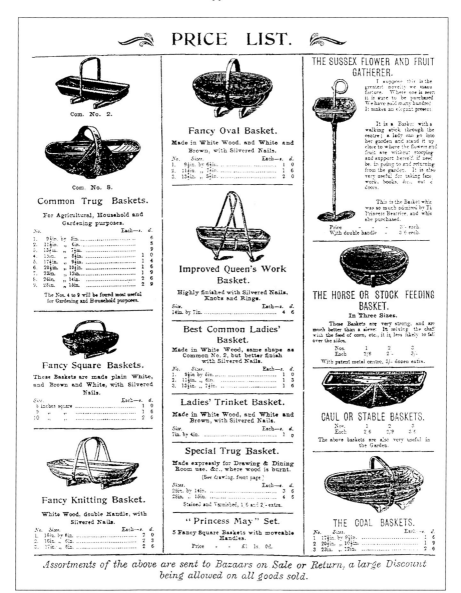

PRICE LIST.

Com. No. 2.

Com. No. 8.

Common Trug Baskets.

For Agricultural, Household and Gardening purposes.

No.		Each—s.	d.
1.	9½in. by 5in.		6
2.	11½in. „ 6in.		8
3.	13½in. „ 7½in.		9
4.	15in. „ 8½in.	1	0
5.	17½in. „ 9½in.	1	4
6.	20½in. „ 10½in.	1	6
7.	23in. „ 12in.	1	9
8.	26in. „ 14in.	2	6
9.	28in. „ 16in.	2	9

The Nos. 4 to 9 will be found most useful for Gardening and Household purposes.

Fancy Square Baskets.

These Baskets are made plain White, and Brown and White, with Silvered Nails.

Size.	Each—s.	d.
8 inches square	1	0
9 „ „	1	6
10 „ „	2	0

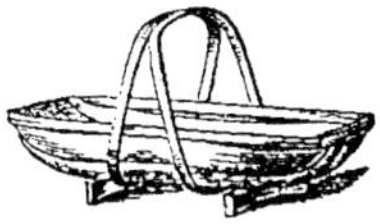

Fancy Knitting Basket.

White Wood, double Handle, with Silvered Nails.

No.	Sizes.	Each—s.	d.
1.	16in. by 6in.	2	0
2.	16in. „ 6in.	2	3
3.	17in. „ 6in.	2	6

Fancy Oval Basket.

Made in White Wood, and White and Brown, with Silvered Nails.

No.	Sizes.	Each—s.	d.
1.	9½in. by 6½in.	1	0
2.	11½in. „ 7½in.	1	6
3.	13½in. „ 8½in.	2	0

Improved Queen's Work Basket.

Highly finished with Silvered Nails, Knobs and Rings.

Size.	Each—s.	d.
14in. by 7in.	4	6

Best Common Ladies' Basket.

Made in White Wood, same shape as Common No. 2, but better finish with Silvered Nails.

No.	Sizes.	Each—s.	d.
1.	9½in by 6in.	1	0
2.	11½in. „ 6in.	1	3
3.	13½in. „ 7½in.	1	6

Ladies' Trinket Basket.

Made in White Wood, and White and Brown, with Silvered Nails.

Size.	Each—s.	d.
7in. by 4in.	1	0

Special Trug Basket.

Made expressly for Drawing & Dining Room use, &c., where wood is burnt.

(See drawing, front page.)

Sizes.	Each—s.	d.
26in. by 14in.	3	6
28in. „ 16in.	4	6

Stained and Varnished, 1/6 and 2/- extra.

"Princess May" Set.

5 Fancy Square Baskets with moveable Handles.

Price - - £1 1s. 0d.

THE SUSSEX FLOWER AND FRUIT GATHERER.

I suppose this is the greatest novelty we manufacture. Where one is seen it is sure to be purchased. We have sold many hundred. It makes an elegant present.

It is a Basket with a walking stick through the centre; a lady can go into her garden and stand it up close to where the flowers and fruit are without stooping and support herself, if need be, in going to and returning from the garden. It is also very useful for taking fancy work, books, &c., out of doors.

This is the Basket which was so much admired by The Princess Beatrice, and which she purchased.

Price - - - 3/- each.
With double handle - 3/6 each.

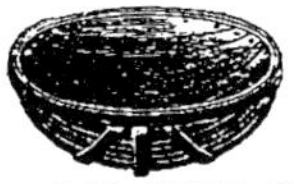

THE HORSE OR STOCK FEEDING BASKET.

In Three Sizes.

These Baskets are very strong, and are much better than a sieve. In mixing the chaff with the feed of corn, etc., it is less likely to fall over the sides.

Nos.	1	2	3
Each	2/6	2/-	3/-

With patent metal centre, 3/- dozen extra.

CAUL OR STABLE BASKETS.

Nos.	1	2	3
Each	2/6	2/9	3/6

The above baskets are also very useful in the Garden.

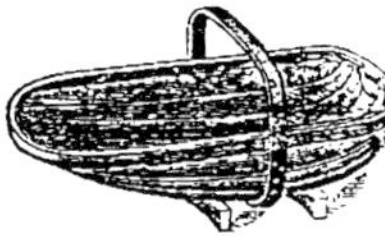

THE COAL BASKETS.

No.	Sizes.	Each—s.	d.
1	17½in. by 9½in.	1	6
2	20½in. „ 10½in.	1	9
3	23in. „ 12in.	2	6

Assortments of the above are sent to Bazaars on Sale or Return, a large Discount being allowed on all goods sold.

Reproduction of an early 20th century price list from Thomas Smith & Sons, Royal Sussex Trug Basket Manufactory, Herstmonceux, near Hailsham.

EARLY GLASS MAKING TECHNIQUES

The manufacture of Crown glass showing the various stages of blowing and rapid whirling, c.1830s.

Making Crown Glass

The first man, called the gatherer, dips the end of his blow-pipe into the molten glass through the furnace mouth. He turns the pipe round until he has gathered a pound or two of pasty glass; he allows it to cool and then dips it again to increase the quantity, repeating the process until he has eight or nine pounds. He then rolls it to and fro on a smooth iron plate (the marver) to give a cylindrical form.

An assistant then blows through the pipe, making the glass into a pear shape. It is then handed to the blower who heats it at the mouth of the furnace two or three times, at each heating blowing and rotating until it is the required size and thickness.

The side of the glass balloon opposite the tube is flattened by being pressed against an iron plate or by being exposed to the heat from the furnace.

The glass is transferred from the pipe to a solid iron rod (the punty). Now it is transformed into a flat circular sheet. The workman holds the punty so that the glass will be exposed to the heat of the furnace at one of the openings called a nose hole. While the glass is exposed to the heat he keeps on rotating. The glass becomes hotter and softer until, yielding to the centrifugal force built up by the rotation, the globe suddenly flashes out into a circular sheet four or five feet in diameter.

The punty is broken away, leaving the characteristic bullion mark in the centre.

Making Broad Glass

The gatherer dipped a long iron pipe into the pot of molten glass and drew out a gather of glass which he then blow into a bubble, (Being careful not to suck in hot air).

The bubble of glass on the end of the blow-pipe was periodically rolled on a flat polished stone known as a marver.

The gathering, smoothing and blowing were repeated until the required size of bubble was formed. Then the bubble was elongated by swinging it to and fro to form a cylinder with rounded ends.

The end of the elongated bubble was softened in the heat of the furnace and pierced by a mallet and peg. The hole was widened out by the procello, large iron tongs. It was then partly cut open.

The cylinder was next transferred from the blow-pipe to the punty (or pontil) a solid iron rod with a wooden disc near the end which held the cylinder in position. The other end could then be cut, reheated and opened as before.

The still hot cylinder was sheared open and flattened. The flat sheets of glass were afterwards put into the annealing kiln where they were left to cool down slowly. The glass produced was slightly wavy and uneven, dulled by the inevitable contact with another surface which occurred during the flattening.

*Model of 16th
century glass
furnace*

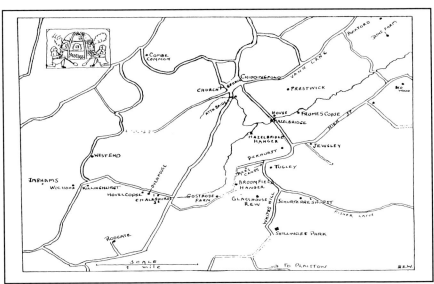

Map showing the Surrey - Sussex glass industry centred around Chiddingfold.

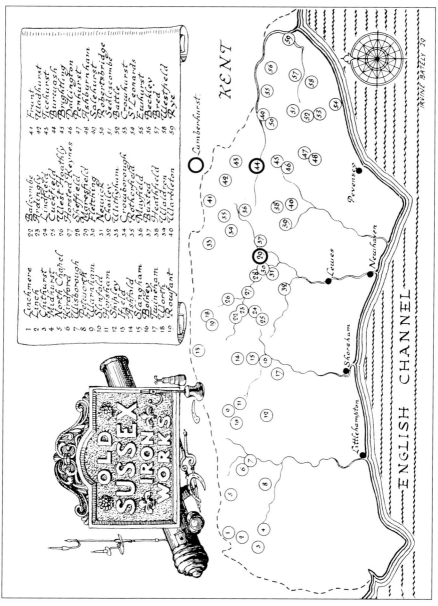

Map illustrating the Sussex iron industry.

DICKER POTTERY, HELLINGLY

The Dicker Pottery, Hellingly, now occupied by the Potters public house.

The Drying Room, The Dicker Pottery.